Sacred
AFFIRMATIONS

Meditations on
Discernment of Spirits

Plus Reflections on
Creation, Presence, Memory, Mercy & Eternity

William M. Watson, SJ

Foreword by Most Rev. Michael C. Barber, SJ

Bishop of The Diocese of Oakland

Other Books by William Watson, SJ

Inviting God into Your Life:
A Practical Guide for Prayer

Forty Weeks:
An Ignatian Path to Christ with Sacred Story Prayer

Sacred Story:
An Ignatian Examen for the Third Millennium

Reflections and Homilies:
The Gonzaga Collection

Sacred Story Rosary:
An Ignatian Way to Pray the Mysteries (Coming Spring 2015)

Sacred Story Press
1401 E Jefferson St., STE 405
Seattle, WA 981222

IMPRIMI POTEST
Rev. Scott R. Santarosa, S.J.

IMPRIMATUR
+ Most Rev. Michael C. Barber, S.J.
Bishop of Oakland

ISBN-13: 978-1507586662
ISBN-10: 1507586663

Dedicated to Our Lady of the Way

Unless otherwise stated Scripture quotations are from the New Revised Standard Version, Copyright © 1989, by the Division of Christian Education of the National Council of the Churches of Christ in the United States of America. Used by permission of the publisher.

Cover and Interior Photography and Design by William M. Watson, SJ

Early Praise for Sacred Story Affirmations

"*Sacred Story Affirmations* provides a beautiful ritual project by which each of us can affirm what is best inside us. As a person who meditates and prays every morning, I will use these affirmations in my ritual process. Others can use them in any moment of happy solitude or personal focus. Teens and growing children can benefit greatly from this book, as well. Fr. Watson has gifted the world with a unique approach to the spiritual process of discernment. Highly recommended!

Michael Gurian, New York Times Bestselling Author of *The Wonder of Boys, The Wonder of Girls* and *The Wonder of Aging.*

In this beautiful little volume Rev. William Watson guides us to faith and strength and love, especially at moments when we may lose connection with those God-given qualities of our nature. Christian in expression, absolutely ecumenical in spirit, *Affirmations* uplifts our soul when we most need that.

Gabor Maté M.D.
Author: *In The Realm of Hungry Ghosts: Close Encounters With Addiction*

DEDICATION

We dedicate this book to every spiritual seeker who has the humility to admit they need help to find the path of light and to steer clear the path of darkness.

May you always find the courage to daily sit still in silence to hear God in your heart.

Make all your decisions in times of great calm and peace and never in times of turmoil and confusion. Do not be afraid!

St. Ignatius, pray for us!

CONTENTS

Reflections on
Creation, Presence, Memory, Mercy & Eternity

FOREWORD

With Pope Francis' election and subsequent popularity, interest in his religious order and background has skyrocketed. He is the first religious order pope elected in over 150 years, and the first Jesuit Pope ever. Given his moving speeches, personality, and eye for the compassionate gesture, people have been asking "Where did he get all this?" "What makes him tick?" Pope Francis is the way he is largely through his training and formation in the Jesuit Order.

The essence of Jesuit spiritual formation is a book of meditations and guidance called the *Spiritual Exercises*, written by the founder of the Jesuits, St. Ignatius Loyola. Young Jesuit novices make the famous 30-day silent retreat praying and meditating following St. Ignatius' direction. But the *Spiritual Exercises* are not just for Jesuits.

The book was written in order to help a person come to know and follow God's will in their lives, *without letting anything else get in the way*. As an integral part of the *Exercises* St. Ignatius composed "Rules for the Discernment of Spirits." These aid the seeker to recognize the movements of the Holy Spirit in one's heart and soul. These "Rules" are unique in the history of Catholic spiritual direction, and to my mind, have never been equaled or surpassed by any other saint or spiritual writer.

Having been a Jesuit for over 40 years, Fr. Watson knows the mind of St. Ignatius. Having devoted the majority of his life using the *Spiritual Exercises* to direct retreats for university students, influential business leaders, and normal folks you'd find in the pew on a Sunday morning, Fr. Watson knows these writings well. The genius of Fr. Watson's book is that he can take these spiritual "Rules for Discernment" written in the 16th Century and make them seem fresh, new and exciting. He accomplishes this while being totally faithful to the original intent of the sainted author.

For example, even if you only read and pray over the first chapter, "Be Not Afraid", this book can change your life. Fr. Watson, like St. Ignatius, has the ability to get inside your thoughts, know what is in there that can stand in the way of your receiving God's love, grace and peace, and help you get rid of the block. I can say that about myself after reading the first chapter. With the many challenges I encounter in being a bishop, fear can easily get the upper hand. Fr. Watson is right. God is not the author of fear. Evil is the author of fear.

What is so attractive about this book is that it can be picked up and used immediately by parishioners and seekers no matter your educational or socio-economic background. In my large diocese I have rich, poor, and in-between parishes begging to begin the 40 Weeks program of prayer and discernment.

People everywhere are *thirsty* for God. They are looking to priests and lay leaders to help them grow in their spiritual lives. It's not enough just to attend weekly Mass – as beautiful an experience as that may be. They want to taste more of the riches of the Catholic spiritual tradition. People have a professional life. They have a family life. They have a social life. As Christians, they are entitled to a *spiritual* life! And we Church leaders need to give it to them. Who else can? This book, when used properly, makes a huge contribution to helping us do that.

One last thing. This book is not "for Catholics only." A growing number of Christians from other denominations are discovering Ignatian Spirituality and loving it. Why? Because it is biblically based. By that I mean St. Ignatius draws lessons for discernment from the Sacred Scriptures and applies them in a practical way to people's lives.

The present book has biblical quotations supporting each of St. Ignatius' and Fr. Watson's principles for discernment. I have friends who are pastors of Presbyterian and Episcopalian churches who are anxious to begin Fr. Watson's *Forty Week's* program in their parishes; the source of the original *Affirmations* phrases in the current volume.

Fr. Watson has done the Catholic Church and the wider Christian community a great service in giving us this volume.

Most Reverend Michael C. Barber, S.J.
Bishop of Oakland

THE AFFIRMATIONS

The Affirmations in this book are thumbnail sketches in spiritual discernment inspired by St. Ignatius of Loyola. They can be a tremendous spiritual resource for your life. Most of them are lifted from St. Ignatius' Rules for the Discernment of Spirits; called Rules for Weeks One and Two in the *Spiritual Exercises*. Week One Rules are more appropriate for understanding how to discern the different spiritual signatures of God and "the enemy of human nature" (St. Ignatius' name for Satan) on the sensual level of life. Week Two Rules are designed to help with understanding the different spiritual signatures of God and the enemy of human nature at the spiritual level and in our intellect.

I have taken the substance of St. Ignatius' "Rules" for both Week One and Week Two and translated Ignatius' discernment guidelines

1

into affirmative statements. Learning their wisdom can provide hope and encouragement on your spiritual journey through this life to Christ's eternal kingdom. You can also avoid much suffering and grief as you learn the predictable ways evil manifests in your life history—your story—and learn to resist the spiritual assaults and deceptions that move you away from the pathway of light.

Because the Affirmations are so important and so beneficial to our spiritual journey, we examine each one and build a prayerful meditation around it to help you better understand its meaning for your own Sacred Story. The Affirmations were written for the book, *Forty Weeks: An Ignatian Path to Christ with Sacred Story Prayer*. Yet they are beneficial for any person of good will seeking to better understand the signals that point to the path of light and resist those that lead to the path of darkness.

In preparation for our Affirmations journey, I invite you to reflectively pray over one Affirmation each week and let its wisdom gradually sink into your mind and heart. All of them are valuable and important and each individual Affirmation will have specific significance at different points in your faith journey. The meaning and value of certain ones will strike your heart immediately while others may not make any sense at all. Don't worry! All of them will eventually make sense and their meaning will only deepen as your spiritual journey unfolds.

Pay attention to those that speak to your heart. As you do, ask God *why* they are meaningful for your own Sacred Story. St. Ignatius always wants us to ask God for the grace of understanding. So don't be shy! Tell the Lord: "this touches my heart - help me to understand why it is important for me in my life." Note too, the ones that made no sense at all on your first pray-through. Ask that God's Holy Spirit keep you open to the graced wisdom they can offer further down the road of your Sacred Story journey.

Lord Jesus, you promised to always be with each of us and with the Church until the end of the age. I pray that you keep me awake to the many helps you provide to me along the journey of life, especially the discernment wisdom in the Affirmations. May this series of spiritual lessons help me to open more fully to Your Creation, Presence, Memory, Mercy and Eternity alive in my heart.

ଔ

The just rejoice and exult before God;
They are glad and rejoice.
Sing to God, chant praise to his name;
Whose name is the Lord.
(Psalm 68: 4-5)

MY SACRED STORY
TAKES A LIFETIME TO WRITE

It is a cliché to say that life is not over till it is over. I doubt anyone would disagree with this fact. Yet often ignored is the fact that we have to work daily on our spiritual growth. Or more precisely, we must work daily to open to the Artist who can transform our lives into a Sacred Story.

Think of your life as a work of art. The powerful image from Jeremiah 18 about the potter and the clay speaks to this: "…Indeed, like clay in the hand of the potter, so are you in my hand, house of Israel." In this passage God reminds Israel that a potter can destroy a bad work of art and rebuild a new one from the original clay. While that might seem a bit harsh to contemplate, we can view the potter and clay image through the lens of Christ Jesus who has come to restore what was lost.

Christ can take our lives, daily undermined by the weight of bad decisions, selfishness, and our own sin and weakness, and transform all of it into blessing. God, in Jesus, is the artist and it will take a complete lifetime for the Lord to work His miracles of grace in our Sacred Story. We will always be in need of the merciful forgiveness of the divine artist in Jesus. Once we see that Jesus needs to work daily in our lives, we understand why "my Sacred Story takes a lifetime to write."

Lord Jesus, you never tire of being our Savior and you never get discouraged with our failures and weaknesses. We give you thanks for your great patience with us and we pray that we allow you, daily, to write our sacred story by your love and grace so that we may praise you in Creation, Presence, Memory, Mercy and Eternity.

ଔ

Teach us to number our days aright,
That we may gain wisdom of heart.
Return, O Lord! How long?
Have pity on your servants!
(Psalm 90: 12-13)

BE NOT AFRAID:
FEAR COMES FROM
THE ENEMY OF MY HUMAN NATURE

The phrases, "be not afraid " and "fear not" are two of the most common phrases in scripture. Fear enters human history after our fall from grace. We did not know fear in our state of original innocence. But we gave into the temptation of "the knowledge of good and evil" and thus, much of our lives are now consumed by fear.

Instilling fear in our hearts is the principal role incarnate evil plays in our lives. The more we fear, the less we trust God. Evil even tricks us into being afraid of God, so we will not turn to God when our need is greatest. We fear God's judgment of us and so we remain isolated and consumed by grief.

We must constantly challenge the fear that rules our lives. We must awaken to the fact that fears just below the surface of consciousness are designed to manipulate our choices and decisions so that we avoid what can bring us hope and peace. We oftentimes do not recognize when we make *or* avoid choices due to fear. We must awaken to evil's strategy of using fear to manipulate us at every possible point in our lives. We must live in trust of God and be not afraid.

Always examine fears and the way they seek to manipulate you. The fear may be focused on giving up some sensual habit that undermines your human nature or a spiritual fear about approaching Confession. God is not the author of fear. Evil is the author of fear. Awaken to fear's destructive ways and be not afraid. Trust in the Lord always!

Lord Jesus, help us unmask the fears that control our hearts and keep us from the joy of more fully serving you. Teach us what we fear and teach us not to be afraid. We thank you for conquering the author of fear so that we may praise you in Creation, Presence, Memory, Mercy and Eternity.

ଔ

Have mercy on me, O God, in your goodness;
In the greatness of your compassion wipe out my offense.
Thoroughly wash me from my guilt
And of my sin cleanse me.
(Psalm 51: 3-4)

THE PATHWAY TO GOD'S PEACE AND HEALING RUNS THROUGH MY HEART'S BROKENNESS, SIN, FEAR, ANGER AND GRIEF

The human story is forever transformed when our first parents made the choice to turn their hearts from God. This sin, apart from ending our immortality, broke our hearts and robbed us of peace. The world of perfect relationship ended and the world of broken relationships began. When perfect relationship ends, the relationships our hearts were made to receive are opened to grief, shame, anger and death.

But God would not tolerate the destruction of His beautiful creation nor the beautiful creatures made in the Divine image. He inaugurates the grand rescue operation that culminates in the birth of the messiah. The Lord Jesus enters into our broken world and into the chaos and darkness of the evil occasioned by our choice to reject God. Indeed, He bears the full weight of the destruction of the relational world and is consumed by it as He enters our experience of abandonment: "...And about three o'clock Jesus cried out in a loud voice, 'eli, eli, lema sabachthani?' Which means, 'my God, my God, why have you forsaken me?'" (Mt 27: 46).

If you want to be holy, you must allow the Divine Physician to enter into your sinfulness, brokenness, fear, anger and grief—all that relates to the imperfect, unbeautiful and shameful dimensions of your human story. It is the Divine Physician's intention to transform the ugliness of our sin and grief into blessings and peace. The Father transformed the scandal of the cross into our resurrection. Christ will transform the scandal and shame of our brokenness into our joy and our hope.

Lord Jesus, give us the courage to let you into the brokenness of our hearts and history. By your grace working in the wounds of our lives, we believe you will transform them into a sacred story and in this we may praise you forever in
Creation, Presence, Memory, Mercy and Eternity.

附

He raises up the lowly from the dust;
From the dunghill he lifts up the poor
To seat them with princes,
With the princes of his own people.
Praise the Lord who lifts up the poor.
(Psalm 113: 7-8)

GOD RESOLVES ALL MY PROBLEMS
WITH TIME AND PATIENCE

The enemy of human nature is fond of using our impatience to generate great worry and anxiety. When we are worried and anxious, we turn our eyes away from the Lord. We focus almost exclusively on our problems, whether they are great or small. We forget all the times the Lord has rescued us in the past. We think, "why is this happening to me? Where is God?" The enemy's strategy, shrewdly implemented, is to keep us focused on the difficulty of any situation, seeing only its seeming hopelessness. This strategy keeps us from turning to the Lord who, in time, rescues us; always, always, always, rescues us!

When you find yourself getting tied up in knots over your problems, turn to God and praise the Lord for all the times you have been rescued in the past. Thank Christ Jesus, and tell him, "you are my Savior, you always help me. I trust you to help me resolve these problems. Please keep me patient as your grace works. Keep my heart focused on your love and fidelity. Lord I thank you for the marvelous way you will resolve this present crisis. Thank you!"

Lord Jesus, you have been our refuge from one generation to the next. You are faithful to your people and the church. You never leave us. Make us turn to you in our trials that we may praise you forever in Creation, Presence, Memory, Mercy and Eternity.

℘

Be still before the Lord; wait for him.
Wait a little, and the wicked will be no more;
Look for them and they will not be there.
But the poor will inherit the earth,
Will delight in great prosperity.
(Psalm 37: 7, 10-11)

I WILL HAVE DIFFICULTIES IN THIS LIFE

The grandfather of all modern self-help books is M. Scott Peck's *The Road Less Traveled*. It took five years to become a New York times bestseller but once it did, it stayed on the list, often at #1, for 694 weeks. The opening line of the book is, "Life is difficult." Obviously the message struck a chord with millions of people, and the message that self-discipline is required to tackle life's challenges did too. People, Peck once said, try to avoid difficulties and it only makes life more difficult.

It should be noted that the book also challenged the prevailing mood that life should not be difficult. We can often be upset that we have difficulties in life, but they are present nonetheless. We either choose to avoid them or deal with them. The original sin guaranteed that life would be difficult. Yet the advent of God's saving mission in Christ provides a super-guarantee that through those difficulties, grace and love will triumph.

We never face our difficulties alone. We have Christ, daily present to us in the power of the Holy Spirit and in the Eucharist. Both forms of "presence" bring us hope and comfort. He promised to stay with us "until the end of the age," and His promise is true (Mt 28: 20).

Lord Jesus, you endured all the pains and difficulties of life to free us from the burden of sin. Thank you for your gift of presence to us.
May we seek you often in the Eucharist and by helping our brothers and sisters in distress, so that one day we may all praise you in Creation, Presence, Memory, Mercy and Eternity.

ʚɞ

"Will the Lord reject us forever, never again show favor?
Has God's mercy ceased forever?
The promise to go unfulfilled for future ages?"
I will recall the deeds of the Lord; yes, recall your wonders of old. I will ponder all your works; on your exploits I will meditate.
(Psalm 77: 8-9; 12-13)

THERE ARE JUST TWO WAYS TO COPE
WITH MY DIFFICULTIES
ONE LEADS TO LIFE, ONE TO DEATH
I WILL CHOOSE LIFE

The Lord's labor of love to rescue and redeem humanity begins by calling a people and giving them the code of our true human nature. The code of the Ten Commandments is a gift to help them discern truth from falsehood in all their relationships. Once given the law of relationships, they are cautioned: *I have set before you life and death, the blessing and the curse. Choose life, then, that you and your descendants may live, by loving the Lord, your God, obeying his voice, and holding fast to him. For that will mean life for you, a long life for you to live on the land which the Lord swore to your ancestors, to Abraham, Isaac, and Jacob, to give to them.* (Dt 30: 19-20).

Life is difficult, as we have already reflected. But knowing the right path to choose in the face of life's difficulties is often less complicated than we think. There may appear to be thousands of options, but in fact there are only two options for each decision. We can choose life or death. We can choose love or retribution. We can choose forgiveness or hate. We can choose humility or pride. We can choose generosity or selfishness. We can choose to turn towards God or to turn away. We can choose hope or despair.

We affirm that we have a choice in each and every decision. Let us always see the choices that lead to life and ask God for the grace to open to the light.

Lord Jesus, you have been our hope from one generation to the next. You never leave our side. Strengthen us to always reject choices that lead to death and choose instead those that lead to life, so that each decision in in my sacred story opens to
Creation, Presence, Memory, Mercy and Eternity.

❧

The Lord has made his salvation known:
In the sight of the nations he has revealed his justice.
He has remembered his kindness and his faithfulness
Toward the house of Israel.
(Psalm 98: 2-3)

"IMPOSSIBLE" IS NOT A WORD IN GOD'S VOCABULARY

Throughout scripture, numerous stories testify to *this* truth: in the end, no obstacle can stand against God's mercy, truth, justice, peace and love. Sin, betrayal, deceit, treachery, imprisonment, slavery, captivity, injustice, barrenness, poverty, natural disasters, sickness and even death—nothing can prevent the love of God from reaching its fulfillment for our salvation.

When we pray the Rosary, we remember that with God, all things are possible: *Then the angel said to her, "do not be afraid, Mary, for you have found favor with God...for nothing will be impossible for God.* (Lk 1: 30-31, 37).

It is of vital importance that we hold fast to this biblical faith in God's power. We must remember that nothing is impossible for God especially when we face those situations that appear from our perspective unsolvable. I think this faith in God's triumphant love is why Pope Francis has such affection for "Mary, the untier of knots." God, working through Mary and many other parts of the body of Christ, does indeed untie all knots—no matter how twisted and tight!

Consciously bring your most "unsolvable and impossible" situations to God. Surrender them with absolute faith and confidence that God will help you. Activate your faith ahead of time and praise God's power and victory over these situations—your hope will increase and your spirits will be lifted up. Do not be afraid, for nothing is impossible for God!

Lord Jesus, you endured all the pains and difficulties of life to free us from the burden of sin. Thank you for your gift of presence to us. May we seek you often in the Eucharist, and recognize you in our distressed brothers and sisters, so that one day we may all praise you in Creation, Presence, Memory, Mercy and Eternity.

ଔ

The Lord is your guardian; the Lord is your shade;
He is beside you at your right hand.
The sun shall not harm you by day, nor the moon by night.
(Psalm 121: 5-6)

SACRED STORY LEADS TO MY FREEDOM AND AUTHENTICITY, BUT DOES NOT ALWAYS MAKE ME FEEL HAPPY

Jesus told us that if we "remained in [His] word", we would be true disciples: *you will know the truth, and the truth will set you free.* (Jn 8:32). Each of us has had a faith-inspired experience of a truth that challenges previously held convictions. The new "true belief" or "true practice" that we have discovered brings freedom. But it can also bring discomfort because it upsets our established patterns.

Think of the call of Simon Peter (Lk 5:1-11). The fisherman "sees the truth" that Jesus is Lord in the incident of the miraculous catch of fish. But in this true vision, he also sees himself as he is: *depart from me Lord, for I am a sinful man.* Jesus brings Peter freedom to see rightly, which reveals his true lack of freedom.

Following Jesus to live a life as Sacred Story leads to my authenticity and freedom. But it might also bring discomfort as the light of Christ shines brightly on the places in my life history—my beliefs and practices—that need reform and change.

We must never confuse the true peace of following the Lord with the false peace or shallow happiness of clinging to beliefs and practices that, even though familiar, are not serving our true freedom. We must shoulder the discomfort of spiritual growth that brings us freedom and thank the Lord for calling us to live authentically.

Lord Jesus, give us patience with our spiritual growth. Let us not be discouraged by the spiritual and emotional discomfort when you call us to grow in freedom and authenticity. Give us happiness and true peace as we grow into living our lives as a sacred story. Gives us the true freedom that opens us to Creation, Presence, Memory, Mercy and Eternity.

ೞ

The Lord confronts the evildoers,
To destroy remembrance of them from the earth.
When the just cry out, the Lord hears them,
And from all their distress he rescues them.
(Psalm 34: 17-18)

MY LIFE'S GREATEST TRAGEDIES CAN BE TRANSFORMED INTO MY LIFE'S MAJOR BLESSINGS

It is important to listen to the phrasing of this Affirmation. The "can" in "can be transformed" does not limit the *capability* of God. It indicates the possibility of transformation that relies on *my cooperation* with God's grace. There is nothing that God cannot transform. No tragedy, disaster or hopeless case is beyond God's power. But the "can" indicates that God needs my active faith and cooperation to work His miraculous transformations.

As difficult as it might be at the time of some personal misfortune or tragedy, we must have the presence of heart to turn to God and call upon His graces to bring light out of darkness. But we are invited to go even further than this. We should begin to thank God for the ways in which these events, that seem like "the end of the world," will be transformed to my benefit by the miraculous grace of God.

If we begin with the "sacrifice of praise" at the moment of some misfortune, we begin to activate our faith in the God for whom "nothing is impossible" (Lk 1:37). Our spirits can be lifted up, even in great misfortune, and we can be restored to a measure of interior peace and hope. Be not afraid: *I have told you this so that you might have peace in me. In the world you will have trouble, but take courage, I have conquered the world.* (Jn 16: 33).

Lord Jesus, I affirm that you are the Lord of life. All sickness, disasters, and misfortunes—yes even death itself—are transformed by your redeeming love. Give me the grace to open my heart to you, especially at times of great misfortune, so that you can work your miracles of grace in my life and the lives of those I love. May even the greatest misfortunes eventually be transformed into your
Creation, Presence, Memory, Mercy and Eternity.

ଔ

The Lord is faithful in all his words
And holy in all his works.
The Lord lifts up all who are falling
And raises up all who are bowed down.
(Psalm 145: 13,14)

TIMES OF PEACE AND HOPE
ALWAYS GIVE WAY
TO TIMES OF DIFFICULTY AND STRESS

Times of spiritual blessing and peace are to be savored. They should call forth from us joy in God's abundant goodness. We need to very consciously attend to the blessings we are receiving. We grow in faith when we make a point of thanking God for the blessings of hope, peace, joy, love, reconciliation and whatever else we might be enjoying as *gift* from the Lord.

When we are clothed by blessings and grace, we can hardly remember times of difficulty or pain. They are swept away by joy (Jn 16: 21). These times of abundant blessing and peace, although they point to our final destiny, are never permanent in this life. We do well to remember in times of blessing that all is gift from God. We do well also in these moments to ask God for strength and fortitude for the next time of difficulty that lies in the future.

By honoring God in times of abundance and reminding ourselves to hold fast in times of future stress, we entrust our whole life to God. And we are ensuring that when misfortune again makes itself felt, we will not be undone by it. For we have already reminded ourselves that all is gift from God. It is this same God who will one day make that joy and peace permanent.

Lord Jesus, may we never fail to praise you in times of great joy, blessing and peace for it is you who are our anchor in this life. Keep our hearts anchored in you so that whether we experience joy or sorrow, we know you are our source and end—our Creation, Presence, Memory, Mercy and Eternity.

಄

My steps have been steadfast in your paths,
My feet have not faltered.
I call upon you, for you will answer me, o God;
Incline your ear to me; hear my word.
(Psalm 17: 5-6)

TIMES OF DIFFICULTY AND STRESS ALWAYS GIVE WAY TO TIMES OF PEACE AND HOPE

Anyone who has been sick with the flu or a severe cold knows how sickness diminishes one's perspective and limits it to the present misery. When we try to recall the feeling of health in the midst of our sickness, it seems completely foreign! Just as physical misery destroys our perspective, so does spiritual distress. When we suffer a loss of faith, hope and love, we can feel like life has ended—that it was never good and will never be good again!

The enemy of our human nature seeks to instill fear during these times of spiritual desolation. He knows we will be susceptible to rash judgments and he wants us not to lose hope. So during these times of "spiritual desolation" we must consciously turn our hearts and minds to God. We must make an act of faith that grace, light, hope and peace will return and that God has not forgotten us. We must activate our spiritual energies and even though we don't feel hopeful, we must make a firm act of faith that hope, peace, and joy will return.

Lord Jesus, let us know that you walk beside us in times of trial and temptation . When our hope has fled, be our stronghold. Make us turn our hearts to you and give us the conviction that you will give us a future of hope and peace. Even though we may feel a loss of faith, hope and love, let us remember that you have never allowed us to be tested beyond our strength. May we turn our hearts to you in all our troubles, you who are our Creation, Presence, Memory, Mercy and Eternity.

ଔ

*"Be still and know that I am God!
I am exalted among the nations, exalted on the earth."
The Lord of hosts is with us;
Our stronghold is the God of Jacob.
(Psalm 46: 11-12)*

I WILL NOT TIRE OF ASKING GOD FOR HELP SINCE GOD DELIGHTS IN MY ASKING

The first Sunday Angelus address of Pope Francis was delivered to the people of Rome on March 17, 2013. It was the Lenten season and the Pope was speaking about God and forgiveness. He said:

"Let us not forget this word: God never tires of forgiving us, never! 'So, father, what is the problem?' Well, the problem is that we get tired, we don't want to, we get tired of asking forgiveness. Let us never get tired. Let us never get tired."

The Lord never tires of us asking for forgiveness. We have emphasized this truth in an earlier Affirmation. But it is not limited to forgiveness - the Lord never tires of us asking for help, no matter what the need is!

At times, I am amazed at how often I forget to ask God for help. Yet when I do, God always, always, always helps. Many times the Lord helps me in unexpected ways, but it is always better than what I had expected.

Why do we fail to ask for God's help? Sometimes, we may think that others' problems are much more pressing than ours and we don't want to "bother God". This is a very common thought, but I suspect that this excuse is a form of false humility. At other times, we may be angry with God for the difficulties we face. This anger blocks us from requesting God's help. Still other times, we may feel hopeless - as if nothing will be able to help us. We give up hope and so do not ask for help.

No matter what excuses we use, we must resist our false humility, our angers and our loss of hope and always, always, always ask God to help us. God delights in helping us and His heart goes out to us in our need. Daily ask God for help and begin thanking God daily for hearing your prayer, and for the wonderful fidelity He will display in coming to your rescue.

Lord Jesus, may we always ask for your help and so more fully
experience your love in
Creation, Presence, Memory, Mercy and Eternity.

03

I rejoiced because they said to me,
"we will go up to the house of the Lord."

And now we have set foot
Within your gates, O Jerusalem.
(Psalm 122: 1-2)

THE URGE TO STOP
SACRED STORY PRACTICE
ALWAYS COMES BEFORE
MY GREATEST BREAKTHROUGHS

Early in his conversion, St. Ignatius was confronted with two distinct *discouragement temptations* that he recorded in his autobiography. One was wondering how he could keep to a path of Christian living for the remainder of his life. The other was disgust for his overly zealous religious practices that were exhausting him.

The first discouragement was linked to the panic of giving up his former vices; the second discouragement was linked to his pride in light of his inability to master his sinfulness by only his own effort. The first was a temptation linked to sensual sin and the second was a temptation linked to spiritual sin.

As your own conversion deepens, you will confront similar discouragements. Some will be inspired by the fear of surrendering past pleasures, others will be linked to angers and frustrations at how slowly you find change happening in your life.

Both temptations are "designed" by the enemy of human nature to turn you away from God and the practice of your faith. Be on the lookout for such temptations and resist them! The fact you have them are clear signs that you are on the right track, and by God's grace achieving significant spiritual growth.

Lord Jesus, keep us alert to the temptations of discouragement used by human nature's enemy. Give us the grace to hold fast by your grace to the practice of prayer and spiritual disciplines. May our fidelity in times of temptation and discouragement lead us to you in Creation, Presence, Memory, Mercy and Eternity.

ଔ

Pray for the peace of Jerusalem!
May those who love you prosper!
May peace be within your walls,
Prosperity in your buildings.
(Psalm 122: 6-7)

GOD GIVES ME INSIGHTS, NOT BECAUSE I AM BETTER THAN OTHERS, BUT BECAUSE I AM LOVED

Those engaged actively in their spiritual growth frequently experience graced insights of understanding and wisdom that move them forward in holiness. Some of these insights are profound. Yet we must not allow these gifts to cause pride. God helps us along the way because God *loves* us and because we *need* it, not because we are better than others. Be ever watchful for spiritual pride. It is the greatest threat to our spiritual growth!

Lord Jesus, keep us grateful for the graces of the father. May we not confuse these loving gifts as signs that we have achieved holiness but rather recognize them as aids in our path toward holiness. Keep pride far from our hearts so that in all things we remain open to you, in
Creation, Presence, Memory, Mercy and Eternity.

May his name be blessed forever;
As long as the sun his name shall remain.
In him shall all the tribes of the earth be blessed;
All the nations shall proclaim his happiness.
Justice shall flourish in his time,
and fullness of peace forever.
(Psalm 72: 17)

THE INSIGHTS AND GRACES I NEED TO MOVE FORWARD IN LIFE'S JOURNEY UNFOLD AT THE RIGHT TIME

The last words of Jesus in Matthew's gospel always bring me great joy:

Go, therefore and make disciples of all nations, baptizing them in the name of the father, and of the son, and of the holy spirit, teaching them to observe all that I have commanded you. And behold, I am with you always, until the end of the age. (Mt 28: 19-20.)

Each of us must learn as we advance in our spiritual lives that the Lord never leaves us orphans. We learn, gradually and not without anxiety, that the Lord always gives us what we need, and at just the time we need it. Learning to trust the Lord and to resist doubt is part of the purifying fires that burn away our self-centeredness. We must also learn, as we are called to make disciples of all nations, that the Lord will give us the resources we need for the task.

I remember a story of Mother Theresa of Calcutta on one of her visits in the United States. A Catholic non-profit organization was strapped for cash and told mother about their problems. She asked them who their patron was and they said St. Joseph. She asked them if they had requested his help and they said, "no." On her inspiration and embarrassed they had so little faith, they prayed to St. Joseph and the money they needed was donated the next day.

The Lord watches out for us in our personal lives and in all our apostolic works. His grace and blessings will always come through.

Lord Jesus, may we always take the necessary spiritual risks.
May we learn to trust that you will provide the grace and
support we need at each step of the way. Move us beyond our
complacency and always come to our aid so we can praise you in
Creation, Presence, Memory, Mercy and Eternity.

ଉଚ୍ଚ

The Lord God keeps faith forever,
Secures justice for the oppressed,
Gives food to the hungry.
The Lord sets captives free.
(Psalm 146: 6-7)

MY PERSONAL ENGAGEMENT WITH SACRED STORY ACCOMPLISHES, THROUGH CHRIST, A WORK OF ETERNAL SIGNIFICANCE

In 1985, the American pop artist Andy Warhol said "In the future, everyone will be world-famous for 15 minutes." Of course, the pop artist was speaking about the disposability of modern life and the ease of capturing the world's attention for short-lived fame.

How different is the focus in scripture where in 1 John 2:17 we hear: "Yet the world and its enticement are passing away. But whoever does the will of God remains forever." It is easy to lose sight of the truth that our holy actions—love, forgiveness, charity, kindness, patience, long-suffering, self-sacrifice—apparently so unimportant to the world, are the only actions that will endure to eternity.

Taking time to pray daily and open our hearts to God can feel like a waste of time and appear insignificant in the face of all the pressures and responsibilities of life. Yet when we open to Christ daily in prayer to receive the grace to align our thoughts, words and deeds with Christ, we will "produce results" that endure to eternity.

We must recover a sense of this holy *delayed gratification* and realize our true treasure lies in the world to come. When we work for fruit that endures, we will be eternally famous in the Kingdom of the Father and eternally cherished by Christ Jesus our brother and Lord.

Lord Jesus, help us to judge wisely the things of this earth and to place our hope in the true gifts of the Kingdom to come so we can praise you in
Creation, Presence, Memory, Mercy and Eternity.

ः

The Lord's are the earth and its fullness;
The world and those who dwell in it.
For he founded it upon the seas
And established it upon the rivers.
Let the Lord enter; he is king of glory.
(Psalm 24: 1-2)

INSPIRATIONS CAN HAVE A DIVINE OR A DEMONIC SOURCE I PRAY FOR THE GRACE TO REMEMBER HOW TO DISCERN ONE FROM THE OTHER

All of us are familiar with the cartoon image of a person with an angel on one shoulder and a devil on the other. Each "spirit" is whispering into the person's ear, and presumably with a different message for the individual in question.

The work of spiritual discernment (and it *is* work) calls us to awaken to the two different types of inspiration and notice the directions in which they lead. Those whisperings are not periodic but constant, each seeking to influence our thoughts, words and deeds—one for life and one for death.

This Affirmation invites us to "remember" how to discern

one from the other. We say "remember" because God has placed the truth in our hearts:

For this command which I am giving you today is not too wondrous or remote for you. It is not in the heavens, that you should say, "who will go up to the heavens to get it for us and tell us of it, that we may do it?" Nor is it across the sea, that you should say, "who will cross the sea to get it for us and tell us of it, that we may do it?" No, it is something very near to you, in your mouth and in your heart, to do it. (Dt. 30: 11-14)

Therefore, learning right from wrong is a process of prayerful remembering, for God has placed in our hearts the truth we need to follow to find life and hope.

Lord Jesus, give us the presence of mind and heart to cultivate a deep remembering of your love in our hearts. May your grace help us to learn discernment so that in everything we may praise you in Creation, Presence, Memory, Mercy and Eternity.

☙

Behold, thus is the man blessed who fears the Lord.
The Lord bless you from Zion:
May you see the prosperity of Jerusalem
All the days of your life.
(Psalm 128: 4-5)

CHRIST, WHO HAS WALKED BEFORE ME, SHARES MY EVERY BURDEN

Suffering, whether it is spiritual, psychological or physical is intensified when the one who suffers feels alone, as if no one else understands what they are experiencing. This terrible sense of isolation is the result of sin's fracturing of relationship.

The divine creator knew the terrible suffering that would result if the beloved children divided their hearts and broke relationship with God. Fully anticipating this devastation, the enemy of human nature soothed with deceptive assurances: *You certainly will not die! God knows well that when you eat of it your eyes will be opened and you will be like gods, who know good and evil.* (Gn 3: 4-5).

God's responds to the cataclysm of sin's suffering and

loneliness by fully entering into the suffering created by our own rejection of God's love. The one "for whom and through whom" all creation was made, in an act of supreme love and humility, choose to be born as one of us and to take on the full cost of our sin.

The Lord Jesus wanted us to know, even in the depths of our suffering, that love has come to rescue us and His sacred heart fully understands what we endure. He does not want us to ever feel alone in our suffering, for He is by our side.

Lord Jesus, no matter what we suffer in our lives, give us the presence of mind and heart to always invite you in to our hearts and ask for your help. You know the full depth of our suffering - give us the knowledge of the gift of your love, that we may praise you in
Creation, Presence, Memory, Mercy and Eternity.

 CB

For he shall rescue the poor when he cries out,
And the afflicted when he has no one to help him.
He shall have pity for the lowly and the poor;
The lives of the poor he shall save.
(Psalm 72: 12-13)

CHRIST, WHO HAS WALKED BEFORE ME, WILL HELP ME RESOLVE EVERY CRISIS

The visitation to Mary proclaims God's power to bring about the new heavens and the new earth. The angel Gabriel announces to the world at the fullness of time that the miraculous power of God is coming into the world. The heart of the announcement is this: "For nothing will be impossible for God." (Lk 1: 37)

We must remember at all times that no matter what happens, and no matter how impossible the problems we face, that "nothing will be impossible for God." Christ has promised to resolve all problems by His power and grace and by our patience. We must nurture our faith and give Christ the room to work miracles. Our belief in God's power strengthens us and gives us hope. Faith is a verb and we need to thank God in Christ for the amazing ways He saves us, the church and the world.

Begin again your habit of praise today because Christ, who has walked before all of us, will resolve every crisis to the glory of His Father.

Lord Jesus Christ, we praise you, for you have done wonderful things. Thank you for being our savior and walking ahead of us. Thank you for your promise that for you, nothing will be impossible. Please deepen our faith in your promise so that in everything we may praise you in
Creation, Presence, Memory, Mercy and Eternity.

⃝ଓ

The God of glory thunders,
And in his temple all say, "glory!"
The Lord is enthroned above the flood;
The Lord is enthroned as king forever.
(Psalm 29: 9-10)

CHRIST, WHO HAS WALKED BEFORE ME, KNOWS MY EVERY HOPE

The Lord Jesus knows all our hopes because He is the source of those hopes. He will bring them to pass. Whenever we think that love is not possible, that we will never contribute anything of value to the world, that our time and our luck has run out - whenever we succumb to this darkness, we must find that spark of hope deep in our hearts and realize that God will be faithful. God *will* be faithful and our hope is not in vain. For Christ who has walked before me, knows my every hope, and will bring them to pass in ways unimaginable.

St Therese of Lisieux wrote that the very fact that we have holy desires means that God intends to fulfill them. In other words, God has placed those holy desires in our hearts and they will come to pass because of God's power. This simple message has always deeply moved me and given me hope when I am tempted to doubt. This assurance awakens me to the falsehood of my fears and to the truth of God's promise to save, to bind up, to bring about for all of us a new heavens and a new earth .

Lord Jesus Christ, you are the source and the ultimate object of our hope. Thank you for guaranteeing that our hearts desires will be fulfilled by you. Thank you for being our savior. Let us always hold fast to hope and in this we will find you always in Creation, Presence, Memory, Mercy and Eternity.

ଔ

I have waited, waited for the Lord,
And he stooped toward me and heard my cry.
And he put a new song into my mouth,
A hymn to our God.
(Psalm 40: 2)

CHRIST, WHO HAS WALKED BEFORE ME, KNOWS EVERYTHING I SUFFER

During the cold war, an American Jesuit named Walter Ciszek was captured by the Soviets and charged as a spy. He suffered for years in solitary confinement. They interrogated him night and day until after four years, he broke down and signed a confession that he was guilty.

Fiercely proud, he had built his identity on not signing the confession. When he finally broke, he was devastated and filled with darkness and despair. He slowly began to consider Christ in Gethsemane and his own aloneness and abandonment. Suddenly, Fr. Ciszek felt comforted and realized that Christ understood his suffering.

There is no human suffering that Christ has not personally tasted. We experience great abandonment in those moments when it seems no one can understand our own unique circumstances and pain. Yet, Christ was born, lived and died so that we would never be alone again—so that we would be forgiven and one day find life eternal with him. Christ has walked before us so that we would know that in all things, He understands our grief, suffering and pain, and even in these, is close to our hearts.

Lord Jesus Christ, out of love for us, you have taken on all the suffering of the world. You have done this willingly, so that we would be freed from all that separates us from you. Thank you for undergoing death so that we can have life. Help us to know that there is nothing in heaven or on earth; nothing above or below; no principality or power that can ever separate us from your love. Be our
Creation, Presence, Memory, Mercy and Eternity.

൦ൔ

The Lord is my light and my salvation;
Whom should I fear?
The Lord is my life's refuge;
Of whom should I be afraid?
(Psalm 27: 1)

CHRIST, WHO WALKS BEFORE ME, WILL ALWAYS LEAD ME HOME TO SAFETY

An Affirmation is something declared to be true; a positive statement or judgment. It is not an opinion. When we affirm "Christ who walks before me will always lead me home to safety," that is a fact—a guarantee.

A close friend of mine, Wanda Spasowski, told me a story. Wanda was the wife of the Polish ambassador to the United States under both presidents Kennedy and Reagan. At a very difficult time in her life, she felt overwhelmed by all the events happening in her personal life and in the Polish nation. She was at the breaking point.

Wanda had a deep faith and had been through many other trials. She reached out to Christ through the intercession of our Lady of Czestochowa, patroness of Poland. She was able to get through the crisis and know that the Lord was always by her side.

Wanda's experience is the same as mine. Never in my life have I been denied help and assistance from the Lord. No matter the trial or crisis; things always end up better than I could have ever possibly hoped for, according to the Lord's timing.

I take great comfort in this truth: that Christ, who suffered everything that we do, knows what we can and cannot endure. He will always rescue us when we call to Him. He is faithful and suffered, died and rose again so we would have faith in His care. He wants us to reach out to Him in every crisis and always have faith in His power to rescue us. He died so we could find our way home.

"Do not let your hearts be troubled. You have faith in God; have faith also in me. In my Father's house there are many dwelling places. If there were not, would I have told you that I am going to prepare a place for you? And if I go and prepare a place for you, I will come back again and take you to myself, so that where I am you also may be. (Jn 14:1-3).

Lord Jesus Christ, you walked the way of life and suffering before us so we would know we are never alone. We affirm our faith in you that you will rescue us in every crisis and difficulty and will always lead us home to safety. Increase our faith in you so that in all things, we may hope in your Creation, Presence, Memory, Mercy and Eternity.

Lift up, O gates, your lintels;
Reach up, you ancient portals,
That the king of glory may come in!
(Psalm 24: 7)

I WILL STRIVE TO CURB TEMPTATIONS TO REACT TO PEOPLE AND EVENTS

In the foreword to *Sacred Story: An Ignatian Examen for the Third Millennium,* Jesuit priest George Aschenbrenner wrote:

> "The most dangerous issue confronting our culture is to learn to deal with violent sudden and explosive impulses. Though we can unhealthily try to squelch these strong feelings, such violent explosives simmer in all our hearts and flail out often beyond our control. Without realizing such explosive power resides within us or without an ability to control such eruptions, we all face disaster.
>
> Learning to control these violent impulses is the greatest challenge facing our families, our culture and our world. Facing, learning and helping to control these

activities can be the most important issue for the examen. In years gone by, often children learned from parents and family how to deal with these attacks. But so much of our family structure has now fallen apart – and all of us are now available to deadly disaster.

The Ignatian examen can provide a faithful human education for simmering emotions, unreflective thoughts and explosive impulses. This is the deep-seated heart of Ignatian examen. Never automatic, it requires gutsy work and tough decisions if we are to avoid the deadly disaster that faces us all."[1]

Lord Jesus Christ, help us to curb our temptations to react to persons and events. Give us the grace to control our tongues and to guard our hearts so we can grow in faith, hope and love so live more fully your
Creation, Presence, Memory, Mercy and Eternity.

ℭ

Light shines through the darkness for the upright;
He is gracious and merciful and just.
Well for the man who is gracious and lends,
Who conducts his affairs with justice.
(Psalm 122: 4-5)

---

[1] William M. Watson, SJ, *Sacred Story: An Ignatian Examen for the Third Millennium* (Seattle: Sacred Story Press, 2012), xxviii-xxix.

I WILL ASK MYSELF WHAT CAUSES MY ANGER AND IRRITATION AT PEOPLE AND EVENTS

Filmmaker Alfred Hitchcock was famous for developing the aerial shot to give dramatic perspective to a movie scene. This camera angle is often called a "bird's eye view."

When you find yourself in the grip of the angers and irritations of daily life, consider rising up to get an aerial shot of your situation. Move out of the heat of the moment. Rise above and step outside yourself to see the situation that is causing your displeasure and resentment with a "bird's eye" perspective.

Stepping outside our aggressive moods takes presence of mind and heart. We are so used to just "feeling" the angers and irritations that we must make a decision to remove ourselves from the passion of the moment and watch ourselves dispassionately.

When you step outside the scene of the moment of passion, you can then ask yourself what is causing you to be upset, angry and irritated. The very act of removing yourself from the scene to watch it "from above" will have the effect of diffusing the emotions so that you can ask for God's grace to enlighten the "eyes of your mind" as to the cause of your anger and irritation. Bring God into the conversation so you can seek the grace of enlightenment.

Try it! You will be amazed by what you discover and how this simple "Affirmation" put into practice will help you advance in your Sacred Story. Appropriately enough, another name for the cinematic angle of "bird's eye view" is "God's eye view"!

Lord Jesus Christ, your gaze is compassion and love. Help us to step outside ourselves when we are angry and irritated so that we can be enlightened by your grace to understand our negative moods. Help us to stop and ask your help so that each day we can open more to
Creation, Presence, Memory, Mercy and Eternity.

 CB

Instruct me, o Lord, in the way of your statutes,
That I may exactly observe them.
Give me discernment, that I may observe your law
And keep it with all my heart.
(Psalm 119: 33-34)

I WILL SEEK TO IDENTIFY THE
SOURCE OF MY ANGER AND IRRITATION

Thomas Merton identifies anger as one of the two capital sins that are the most difficult to purge and control. To complicate matters, many people can also be disconnected from the sources of what makes them angry or lustful.

The previous Affirmation encourages one to turn to Christ and ask for enlightenment as to the immediate cause of a particular anger one experiences in the present moment. This Affirmation asks one to seek the original causes, where they exist, of present angers that can be triggered by the undetected and unresolved original wounds in our lives.

This process of spiritual and emotional excavation is something that takes time. It can only be accomplished by God's grace working in union with our openness to that grace. We must never tire of asking God to help us remember the sources of these original events so that we can better "avoid the near occasions" of the sins they prompt.

Yet we know that God will do the hard work we can't do ourselves. The impact of original sin in our lives is something we will never eliminate but with God's help, we can move toward greater and greater understanding and freedom. God is the one who turns our life into a Sacred Story.

Lord Jesus Christ, you are present to us at each moment of our lives and see our entire history. Help us, with your grace to unlock the history of sin and darkness in our history so we can grow in freedom and peacefulness. Give us the grace of forgiveness so that in all our thoughts, word and deeds we can open to your Creation, Presence, Memory, Mercy and Eternity.

⁜

As far as the east is from the west,
So far has he put our transgressions from us.
As a father has compassion on his children,
So the Lord has compassion on those who fear him.
(Psalm 103: 12-13)

I WILL GIVE THANKS FOR WHAT ANGERS AND UPSETS ME FOR IDENTIFYING THEIR SOURCE WILL HELP TO SET ME FREE

Other Affirmations address the issue of identifying the angers (and lusts) in our lives to minimize their destructive influence. This Affirmation invites you to see the angers and upsets that you experience as opportunities for grace and healing.

We humans are gifted with sense perceptions that are physical, spiritual and emotional. We automatically pull away from hot objects because we know they will burn us. Spiritually, we can become sensitive to inspirations from sources of light and darkness. From this we learn which to avoid and which to welcome.

We can also take our most difficult emotions such as anger, and use them as moments of self-understanding and healing.

The things that make us angry can provide valuable information about what frightens, hurts or damages us. Paying attention to the emotion when it erupts and thanking God for the "emotional perception" it provides, can help you unlock its secrets.

Here is one way to go about this process. First, distance yourself from the immediate emotional reaction by turning to God and thanking God for the gift of your emotional self-awareness. Second, ask God for the grace to understand the origin of the angers so that you can better see the outlines of your life story. Third, ask for deep healing and forgiveness. This forgiveness is both for those individuals you need to forgive, and individuals whose forgiveness you need to seek when your angers have become destructive instead of instructive.

Lord Jesus Christ, thank you for the gift of emotional self-awareness. For even those things that anger us can open our hearts to your grace and deepen our self-understanding. Help us always turn to you in our angers and thank you for the ways you transform them into moments of healing and peace, so that in all things we can live Creation, Presence, Memory, Mercy and Eternity.

☙

With God is my safety and my glory, He is the rock of my strength; my refuge is in God. Trust in him at all times, O my people! Pour out your hearts before him.
(Psalm 62: 8-9)

I WILL STRIVE TO
LISTEN, WATCH AND PRAY;
LISTEN, WATCH AND PRAY.
I WILL LISTEN, WATCH AND PRAY!

I believe Jesus' request for the disciples to stay awake in Gethsemane, to "watch and pray," and St. Paul's exhortation to the Romans to "wake from sleep" are spiritually linked.

"So you could not keep watch with me for one hour? Watch and pray that you may not undergo the test The spirit is willing, but the flesh is weak."
(Mt 26: 40-41)

You know the time; it is the hour now for you to awake from sleep. For our salvation is nearer now than when we first believed.
(Rm 13: 11)

Jesus invites His disciples to stay awake to "see" their salvation being accomplished in His surrender to the Father's will. He wants the disciples to stay awake and watch so they will have an example to imitate in their own lives. Despite its importance, it can be very difficult to "stay awake." Sin and the burdens of life can weary us and cause us to fall asleep. It is hard for us to "see" our lives truthfully and this is why we need to surrender our burdened hearts to God.

St. Paul therefore exhorts the Romans to awake from sleep so that they can see the nearness of salvation. St. Ignatius' daily examen (which we pray as *Sacred Story prayer*) is a call to "wake up." Ignatius wants us to see our lives, the world, and the Lord Jesus with clear eyes. We are invited daily to listen, watch and pray. In our simple daily prayer, we can respond to the exhortation of Christ, echoed by Paul, that we may be more fully awake!

Lord Jesus Christ, give me a persevering spirit so that I can always listen to your voice, watch your example and pray for your help. Help me always to listen, watch and pray so that I can fully awaken to Creation, Presence, Memory, Mercy and Eternity.

ള

Give me back the joy of your salvation,
And a willing spirit sustain in me.
O Lord, open my lips,
And my mouth shall proclaim your praise.
(Psalm 51: 17)

EVERYONE HAS BEEN MORTALLY WOUNDED SPIRITUALLY, PSYCHOLOGICALLY, AND PHYSICALLY BY ORIGINAL SIN AND THE LOSS OF PARADISE

We do well to reflect often on God's gifts. God gifted us "originally" with immortality. We were created to share everlastingly in God's love, the love of each other and the amazing cosmos God fashioned. How we could have turned from God and rejected the gift is captured in the phrase: *the mystery of iniquity.*

The spiritual choice to turn away from God's pure love to the love of self is what we call the original sin. The gift of immortality was replaced by the "new normal:" fractured consciousness, broken hearts, violence, murder, depression, disease and death.

The perfect relationship between body, mind and spirit was made possible by our free choice to be fully united with God. When we turned away, all that made us immortal was fatally destabilized. This Affirmation states that we have all been mortally wounded—spiritually, psychologically and physically. We can reflect on the perfect relationship between these three integral dimensions of the human person as the locus of this mortal wound. For sin ultimately destroys relationships. Sin attacks the heart of God's gift—perfect relationship and perfect love.

Only God, in Christ, can restore what was lost. And so, in love, Christ enters into the history of the world's brokenness to undo what was undone. We must admit the full truth of what was lost if we are to ever fully turn to the source of our salvation.

Lord Jesus Christ, help me to know and honestly admit my brokenness and the loss of my original immortality so that I can turn to you with all my heart and awaken anew through your love and grace to Creation, Presence, Memory, Mercy and Eternity.

 C3

Instruct me, O Lord, in the way of your statutes, That I may exactly observe them. Give me discernment, that I may observe your law And keep it with all my heart. (Psalm 119: 33-34)

JOURNEYING WITH CHRIST TO THE ROOTS OF MY SINS AND ADDICTIONS WILL HELP BREAK THEIR GRIP

This Affirmation continues the good news of the Divine Physician's healing graces in our lives. It can be customary for each of us to avoid a conscious awareness of our own sins and addictions. We fear them, or they embarrass us, or they make us feel powerless or pained or hopeless.

Whatever the reasons we might avoid these parts of our lives, we need to allow Christ the divine physician to enter them with His light and healing graces.

Ignoring the darkness within does not make it go away: quite the contrary. Avoiding our darkness only gives it more control, eroding our hope and intensifying fear, embarrassment, powerlessness and pain.

If the original sin was the act of us turning away from God, the way back to God is to look honestly at our sin, with Christ by our side as divine healer and savior of souls. We are not to fear: "There is no fear in love, but perfect love drives out fear because fear has to do with punishment, and so one who fears is not yet perfect in love" (1 Jn 4:18).

Lord Jesus Christ, enter my darkness and powerlessness and help me untangle the sin and addiction in my life. I know with you by my side that I have nothing to fear, for in your love and mercy I can open to Creation, Presence, Memory, Mercy and Eternity.

ଔ

Come, let us bow down in worship;
Let us kneel before the Lord who made us.
For he is our God,
And we are the people he shepherds, the flock he guides.
(Psalm 95: 6-7)

I WILL NOT WASTE TIME WORRYING
ABOUT MY SINS AND FAILURES

To grow in faith requires of us to put on the mind of Christ when contemplating our sins and failures. First, to "put on Christ" entails that I admit my sin, for to deny it is to "call God a liar" (1 Jn 1: 8-10). Second, to "put on Christ" requires that I have hope and faith in Him to heal me and forgive me. When we constantly fret and worry over our sins and failures, we move away from faith in God. We need to confront this damaging and fruitless type of worry because it destroys our hope and only serves the enemy of our human nature.

We could use humor and remind ourselves that "guilt is the gift that keeps on giving." Constant guilt is a form of worry that reveals less a "holy conscience" and more a self-centeredness and effort at self-salvation. Although it is rarely conscious, when we constantly feel guilty, we act as though this suffering from guilt is all the penance we need. It is a tragic, twisted pride that enslaves us.

Lord Jesus Christ let me have the honesty to know my sin and the maturity of faith to trust you completely as my hope and my salvation. Break any and all patterns of worry and guilt that block my faith in you so that I can open each day to Creation, Presence, Memory, Mercy and Eternity.

ଓ

The Lord is my shepherd; I shall not want.
In verdant pastures he gives me repose;
Beside restful waters he leads me;
He refreshes my soul.
(Psalm 23: 1)

I WILL USE MY TIME WISELY AND ASK GOD TO HELP ME UNDERSTAND THE SOURCE OF MY SINS AND FAILINGS

Previous Affirmations suggested how we must resist obsessive worry about our sins and failings. The Lord's desire is always to help us, not scold us. When we imagine Christ as a harsh schoolmaster, we have not understood His mission or the mercy He comes to lavish on those who have been destroyed by sin's effects... and we waste precious time! We must instead work with the Lord who wants to help us grow. We must remember that He is infinitely patient with our failings and weaknesses. All Christ wants is for us to keep trying, to not lose hope and not waste time fretting!

When we allow our faith to mature, we realize that Christ is our fortress and our rock. We must use our time to speak to Christ from our hearts, and ask His help to grow in understanding and freedom. We cooperate with Christ who is mercy and graciousness, when we ask Him to help us in this process of freedom. He will hear our prayers and help us along the way. Jesus is not the cop in the rearview mirror! Jesus is the captain of our hearts and the one who died for us so that we can have life, and have it abundantly! (Jn 10:10).

Lord Jesus Christ, let me use all of my time asking for your help to understand my life. You are the only one who can unlock the mysteries of my heart. I affirm you are loving and forgiving and want to help me grow in freedom. Let me believe this more deeply each day, so that all my time is well-spent opening to you
in
Creation, Presence, Memory, Mercy and Eternity.

α

If you, O Lord, mark iniquities, Lord, who can stand?
But with you is forgiveness, that you may be revered.
For with the Lord is kindness and with him is plenteous
redemption; And he will redeem Israel from all their iniquities.
(Psalm 130: 3-4, 7-8)

I WILL TRUST THAT CHRIST CAME
TO HEAL ALL MY WOUNDS

Merriam-Webster defines "trust" this way: assured reliance on the character, ability, strength, or truth of someone or something. When we say that we trust that Christ can heal my wounds, it means that we have assurance that He has the strength and the ability to do so!

When we say that Christ has come to heal "all" my wounds, we mean the spiritual, physical, and emotional wounds of our lives. It is our spiritual wounds that are the most important, because they are the root of all other wounds. Remember in the scripture how Jesus confounded the scribes with the case of the paralytic: *He said: "which is easier, to say, 'your sins are forgiven,' or to say, 'rise and walk'? But that you may know that the son of man has authority on earth to forgive sins"—he then said to the paralytic, "rise, pick up your stretcher, and go home." (Mt 9: 5).*

We may want the Lord Jesus to only heal our physical or emotional ailments, but He came for a much greater healing—our full spiritual renewal in Him so that we can once again share eternal life . He is indeed, the Divine Physician. Christ is also the "firstborn of all creation" and the "first born from the dead" (Col 1: 15, 18).

Lord Jesus Christ, I believe, help my unbelief! Let me trust more fully in your healing love and never be afraid to surrender my sins in thoughts, words and deeds to you for healing. I affirm that you have the power to heal me and that because of your passion, death and resurrection, I can rise with you to new life. Increase my trust so that I can live with you in Creation, Presence, Memory, Mercy and Eternity.

ℭ

They divide my garments among them,
And for my vesture they cast lots.
But you, O Lord, be not far from me;
O my help, hasten to aid me.
(Psalm 22: 19-20)

I ALONE CONTROL CHRIST'S ABILITY
TO TRANSFORM MY LIFE
INTO A SACRED STORY

It is a fact that love is only possible if it can be freely rejected. Without the freedom to reject love, every relationship would be one of slavery. But since we are made in God's image and likeness, the freedom to love (or not) is our very birthright.

It is vital to remember this freedom. Ultimately the choice is ours, whether we will allow Christ to transform our lives into Sacred Story or not. Christ will never force us to accept Him in our hearts. Not to invite Love into our lives is sure death, but it is up to us to decide. Because we are made in Love's image and likeness, we will never be happy apart from a relationship with God but we have the freedom to say "no" to it. As St. Augustine said in the Confessions: "O Lord our hearts are restless until they rest in thee."

We also have the freedom to make that "no" definitive. We know this is possible because Jesus said that to willfully sin against the Spirit is a sin that cannot be forgiven (Mk 3: 28-29; Mt 12: 30-32). Sin can be "unforgivable" only because we have the freedom to reject the Spirit. This willful hardening of one's heart was something that Jesus noticed not in the tax collectors and sinners but in the religious leaders—the scribes and the Pharisees. Their hardness of heart manifested itself in their frightening assertion that the mighty works of Jesus came from Satan (Mt 12:22-32).

Let us affirm that we hold the power over what happens in our lives and that we have the power to allow Christ to enter our hearts and by His grace, turn all sadness, darkness, sin and death into life—Sacred Story. Let us daily say "yes" to Christ so that in all things we can participate with Him in Creation, Presence, Memory, Mercy and Eternity.

જી

*The stone which the builders rejected
Has become the cornerstone.
By the Lord has this been done;
It is wonderful in our eyes.
(Psalm 118: 22-23)*

THE PROCESS FOR CHRIST TO TRANSFORM MY LIFE INTO SACRED STORY BEGINS WHEN I ASK FOR THE GRACE TO HONESTLY NAME MY SINS AND ADDICTIONS

Opening our hearts to Christ is a choice only we can make. Christ wants us to open to His love as our creator who now recreates us as our healer, forgiver, redeemer and savior. This means we must bring to Him those parts of our lives that need healing. These are the things from which only He can save us—our sins and sinful addictions—and death!

We must be ever-vigilant in this mission of opening to Christ. We must resist the fear that keeps us from honestly naming sin and addiction for what they are: sources of death and slavery. Yet we must not be afraid of our sins and addictions. Christ Jesus is not afraid of them nor does He take offense at those who honestly turn to Him for healing.

He honors our courage by forgiving and strengthening us.

The Sunday after Easter has been very appropriately named Divine Mercy Sunday. The death and resurrection of Christ has unleashed upon the world the healing graces that can and will bring about the new heavens and the new earth (Is 65: 17; Rev 21: 1). Let us take courage and bring our sins and addictions to the Divine Physician who died so we might "have life and have it more abundantly" (Jn 10: 10).

Lord Jesus Christ, with you by my side, give me the courage and grace to honestly look at my sins and addictions. Help me not to be afraid, for fear comes only from the enemy of my human nature. You love me and only want to heal me. Be my divine physician and flood your mercy in all my wounds so that in you I can be restored in Creation, Presence, Memory, Mercy and Eternity.

ೞ

"The right hand of the Lord has struck with power;
The right hand of the Lord is exalted.
I shall not die, but live,
And declare the works of the Lord."
(Psalm 118: 16-17)

THE PROCESS OF CHRIST TRANSFORMING MY LIFE INTO SACRED STORY CONTINUES WHEN I INVITE HIM TO ILLUMINATE MY NARCISSISM

It is one thing to ask God for the grace to honestly name my sins and addictions. It takes even greater courage to ask that my concealed narcissistic pride be unmasked. Narcissism is incredibly deadly because it makes me both god and center of the universe (Gn 3:5). Ignatius struggled mightily with this narcissism. As he discovered, it infects even the religiously pious and those who aspire to holiness. For evil most effectively conceals itself in a mantle of righteousness.

Narcissism is always about a refusal to worship the one God and instead to worship oneself. Outside of a faith context, narcissism can manifest in the obsession over a temporal good (power, beauty, wealth, prestige, etc.). This form of narcissism can also tempt the religious person! But a person of faith is more likely to be tempted to self-salvation. Narcissism manifests by efforts to fulfill the law "perfectly" - therefore eliminating the need to rely on God as savior and redeemer.

Whatever form narcissism takes in my own life, it must be "revealed" to me by the God who knows my heart and who seeks to free me from the pride that this "original sin" wrought in human history. I must ask God to show me the very specific way I seek to be my own god and how I need to repent and open myself to the true God!

Lord Jesus Christ, I affirm that you and you alone are Lord of my life and of the world. You are the firstborn of creation and the firstborn from the dead. Only you are God. Every knee will one day bend to you as Lord and savior of all (Phil 2:10). Grant me the courage to ask for a gracious and compassionate illumination of my narcissism, so that I can find my way to you in Creation, Presence, Memory, Mercy and Eternity.

ೞ

Therefore my heart is glad and my soul rejoices, My body, too, abides in confidence; Because you will not abandon my soul to the netherworld, Nor will you suffer your faithful one to undergo corruption. (Psalm 116: 9-10)

ONLY GOD'S GRACE AND MERCY
CAN WRITE MY SACRED STORY

We come to the end of our Affirmations with one final admission. We have a profound temptation to make ourselves god. The reason we do this is because it takes humility to admit we cannot save ourselves. It takes a lifetime of courage to daily face the fact that we need the Lord as savior and redeemer. This means that daily we must take up our cross and follow the Lord. This is Good News! Listen again to the words from Luke's gospel:

Then he said to all, "if anyone wishes to come after me, he must deny himself and take up his cross daily and follow me. For whoever wishes to save his life will lose it, but whoever loses his life for my sake will save it. What profit is there for one to gain the whole world yet lose or forfeit himself?" (Lk 9:23-25)

We cannot be holy apart from God. Holiness consists of

daily admitting my need of a savior and turning to the savior of the world.

In this turning to God, I admit my weakness. Weakness is the cross I must daily carry to stay in communion with Christ and His mission of reconciliation for the world. There is a freedom in this, because when I learn that I cannot save myself, this is the moment when I fully turn to the one who wants to carry me to new life. There are a number of sayings that capture this reality: "Let God;" or "Let Go and Let God;" or "Let God be God!"

Jesus is the Good Shepherd who seeks out what is lost and brings us home. I do not have to climb the mountain of the Lord alone. I don't have to save myself! God, in Christ, will write my Sacred Story!

Lord Jesus Christ, you are mercy, you are the true Sacred Story of the universe. In you I place all my fears, all my sins and all my failings. I affirm that it is you who will write my personal Sacred Story. Help me turn to you daily and unburden myself from seeking my own salvation. In all things, be for me Creation, Presence, Memory, Mercy and Eternity.

ೞ

You spread the table before me in the sight of my foes;
You anoint my head with oil; my cup overflows.
Only goodness and kindness follow me all the days of my life;
And I shall dwell in the house of the Lord for years to come.
(Psalm 23: 3-6)

II

Reflections On

CREATION
PRESENCE
MEMORY
MERCY
ETERNITY

PRELUDE

The following reflections on Creation, Presence, Memory, Mercy and Eternity comprise the five movements of the Ignatian Examen reframed for the Sacred Story Prayer discipline. Taken together, they invite a Christian to become conscious of the gift of Creation and the Giver of the gift. Presence calls the heart to attend to the spiritual currents the heart is experiencing and Memory invites a two-level reflection process for how what is experienced is both "of the present moment" and also rooted in past history. Mercy invites the aware heart to seek forgiveness for failure and sins (while also offering forgiveness to those who have sinned against us) and Eternity is a call to look with hope to the future so that one may dedicate all one's thoughts words and deeds to producing fruit that will endure to eternity.

The Ignatian Examen as Sacred Story prayer is a synopsis of the whole of creation and salvation history that when prayed daily, unites an individual believer with Christ Jesus, the Body of Christ the Church and Church's work for universal reconciliation. This cosmic SACRED STORY that each of us is called to participate in is beautifully captured in the opening great hymn of *Dei Verbum*, the document on Divine Revelation for the Second Vatican Council.[2]

God, who through the Word creates all things (see John 1:3) and keeps them in existence, gives men an enduring witness to Himself in created realities (see Rom. 1:19-20). Planning to make known the way of heavenly salvation, He went further and from the start manifested Himself to our first parents. Then after their fall His promise of redemption aroused in them the hope of being saved (see Gen. 3:15) and from that time on He ceaselessly kept the human race in His care, to give eternal life to those who perseveringly do good in search of salvation (see Rom. 2:6-7). Then, at the time He had appointed He called Abraham in order to make of him a great nation (see Gen. 12:2). Through the patriarchs, and after them through Moses and the prophets, He taught this people to acknowledge Himself the one living and true God, provident father and just judge, and to wait for the Savior promised by Him, and in this manner prepared the way for the Gospel down through the centuries.

Then, after speaking in many and varied ways through

---

[2] Documents of the Second Vatican Council. Dogmatic Constitution on the Church: *Dei Verbum*. Chapter 1 § 3-4.

the prophets, "now at last in these days God has spoken to us in His Son" (Heb. 1:1-2). For He sent His Son, the eternal Word, who enlightens all men, so that He might dwell among men and tell them of the innermost being of God (see John 1:1-18). Jesus Christ, therefore, the Word made flesh, was sent as "a man to men." (3) He "speaks the words of God" (John 3:34), and completes the work of salvation which His Father gave Him to do (see John 5:36; John 17:4). To see Jesus is to see His Father (John 14:9). For this reason Jesus perfected revelation by fulfilling it through His whole work of making Himself present and manifesting Himself: through His words and deeds, His signs and wonders, but especially through His death and glorious resurrection from the dead and final sending of the Spirit of truth. Moreover He confirmed with divine testimony what revelation proclaimed, that God is with us to free us from the darkness of sin and death, and to raise us up to life eternal.

The reflections on the following pages are offered so that you may enter more fully in the reality and the graces offered by God in Creation, Presence, Memory, Mercy and Eternity. Be not afraid!

CREATION I

The Sacred Story of creation began thirteen point seven billion years ago, give or take a hundred million years. We have only mapped galaxies out to one hundred million light years; the remaining thirteen point six billion light years to the burst at creation's origins is beyond our *vision*. But all that is "seen and unseen" in the universe came to be…from *nothing*. Time and space was *created!* It was not, and then it was. When you pray with Creation in Sacred Story, think of creation as the beginning of the entire SACRED STORY. Let the awesomeness of this truth create wonder in your heart. Ponder its meaning. Give thanks.

Pray for each other. Pray for the church. Pray for the world.
Live gratitude.
Awaken to Creation, Presence, Memory, Mercy and Eternity.

ଔ

Come, let us sing joyfully to the lord.
Let us come before him with a song of praise,
Joyfully sing out our psalms.

For the lord is the great god, the great king over all gods,
Whose hand holds the depths of the earth;
Who owns the tops of the mountains.
The sea and dry land belong to god,
Who made them, formed them by hand.
(Psalm 95: 1-7)

CREATION II

The Sacred Story of creation had another beginning four point five billion years ago. Earth came into existence: the densest of eight planets of a small solar system in the Orion arm on the outer reaches of the Milky Way Galaxy. A rare combination of events enables this beautiful orb to produce complex intelligent life. We are the perfect distance from the center and edge of our galaxy. Our position enables us to escape the center's dangerous radiation and crowding that would disrupt the delicate orbital axis around our star. If we were any further out however, we would be deficient in the heavy metals produced by the supernovas of the galactic center.

As a small planet, we have a dense, unusually large moon that stabilizes the 23° tilt of earth's rotation axis, holding it steady in this position for millions of years. Without the moon as anchor, Jupiter and Saturn would cause a wild orbit, with massive climate changes and an environment hostile to complex life. Without a planet the size of Jupiter, we would be ten thousand times more exposed to the violent strikes of asteroids and meteors that would sterilize the planet, making it unable to sustain life. There has not been one such strike for two point five billion years.

Earth has had two total ice events; one two point five billion years ago and one five hundred and fifty million years ago. The first ice event created conditions for single cell life to expand. The second event, at the time of the Cambrian explosion, conspired to transform single cell life into complex multi-cellular life. The earth possesses a rare plate tectonics that produces a remarkably stable temperature regulation mechanism, enabling the evolution of complex life.[3]

When you pray with Creation in *Forty Weeks*, remember that earth is indeed rare and beautiful. It makes our lives possible. Let the awesomeness of this truth create wonder in your heart. Ponder its meaning. Give thanks.

Pray for each other. Pray for the Church. Pray for the World. Live Gratitude. Awaken to Creation, Presence, Memory, Mercy and Eternity.

CB

---

[3] Inspired by: *Rare Earth: Why Complex Life is Uncommon in the Universe*, by Peter Ward and Donald Brownlee: Copernicus Publishers, 2003. Ward and Brownlee have both taught at the University of Washington.

You fixed the earth on its foundation,
so it can never be shaken.
The deeps covered it like a garment; above the mountains
stood the waters. You made the moon to mark the seasons;
the sun that knows the hour of its setting.
You bring darkness and night falls.
(Psalm 104: 5-6; 19-20)

CREATION III[4]

In spite of all we know about the human person, science cannot really answer the most basic questions of how life works. How does the mind work? What is DNA? Why/how do cells function the way they do? Why is loving, human physical contact necessary for a baby's physical and mental development? How and why does the immaterial spirit (or mind) powerfully impact the material biochemical processes in our cells and vice versa? Just what is *human nature*, the name our tradition gives to the divinely created unity of body/spirit? How does *human nature* work?

We have a better understanding of life's mechanics, but comprehending why life works the way it does is far beyond our capacities. The more we observe of the body and the mind's workings, the more unbelievable life appears. We can't even

---

[4] Inspired by: *The Cell's Design* by Fazale Rana; *Everything You Need to Feel Go(o)d,* by Candace B. Pert, Ph.D.; *The First Gene*, by David L Abel, Editor; *The Spiritual Brain* by Mario Beauregard; *Touching, The Human Significance of the Skin,* by Ashley Montagu; and personal conversations with Mr. Jim Harding of CODONiS.com.

explain how a minute sequoia seed develops into the largest living thing on earth.

When you pray with Creation in Sacred Story, remember that your human life is a miracle that even the most brilliant scientific minds can't explain. Let the awesomeness of this truth create wonder in your heart. Ponder its meaning. Give thanks.

Pray for each other. Pray for the church.
Pray for the world.
Forgive. Live in gratitude.
Awaken to Creation, Presence, Memory, Mercy and Eternity.

ﻼ

When I see your heavens, the work of your fingers,
The moon and stars that you set in place—
What is man that you are mindful of him,
And a son of man that you care for him?
Yet you have made him little less than a god,
Crowned him with glory and honor.
You have given him rule over the works of your hands,
Put all things at his feet.
(Ps 8: 4-7)

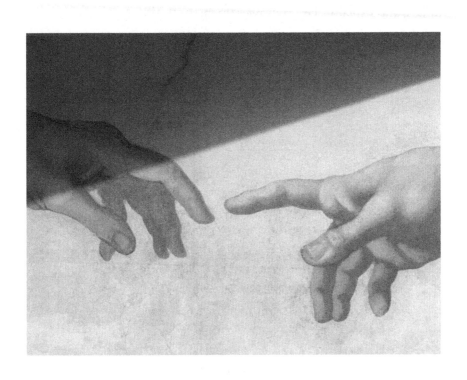

CREATION IV

Scripture affirms that God created the cosmos *ex-nihilo*—from nothing (Gn 1:1). We can affirm that this Divine act of creation was an act of Love. God is Love (1 Jn 4:8). God created human persons, women and men, to share in this love and in love's creative energy. For marital love offers husbands and wives a share in God's loving, creative genius. Of woman and man, a child is born who will live for eternity.

Have you ever contemplated this profound mystery: the creative power God gives to women and men? An eternal being is born in time. When you pray with Creation in Sacred Story, remember that your human life is an *ex-nihilo* act of Love from God through your parents. You did not have to *be*, but Love desired that you be born. Creation is an act of Love. You are born by God's act of Love shared with your parents. Let the awesomeness of this truth create wonder in your heart. Ponder its meaning. Give thanks.

Pray for your parents, be they living or deceased.
Thank God for the life they gave to you.
Choose Gratefulness. Choose Life.
Awaken to Creation, Presence, Memory, Mercy and
Eternity.

ଓଃ

My lover speaks and says to me,
"Arise, my friend, my beautiful one, and come!
For see, the winter is past,
the rains are over and gone.
The flowers appear on the earth,
the time of pruning the vines has come,
and the song of the turtledove is heard in our land."
(Song of Songs 2: 10-12)

CREATION V

If a person had the occasion to ask God *one* question, it might be; "WHY? Why did you create all of this?" Perhaps God's response would be; "Because I thought it would delight you." In the end, we can reach no other conclusion for creation. The remarkable, awesome and beautiful universe we are privileged to delight in was God's *deliberate choice*—a gratuitous gift by Love to share love. It is *all* a gift from Love itself.

Creation is love made visible. *Human beings* are the height of God's creation; persons who can receive God's love and offer love to others. In our loving, we become co-creators with God. Jesus Christ is Love itself poured out in complete humility to be Emmanuel, "*God with us.*" Love, The Infinite One, The Almighty, The Creator of all has become *one of us*! Love itself, sharing Love with us creatures made in Love's

Divine image. We are empowered by Love to create in love, other beings who will also be able to love. Love is the source of all creative energy. Let the awesomeness of this truth create wonder in your heart. Ponder its meaning. Give thanks.

Pray in gratitude for creation's gift—for your life!
Pray to cultivate a grateful heart. Pray for a loving heart.
Pray that Christ's Spirit guides all your
thoughts, words and deeds. Awaken to
Creation, Presence, Memory, Mercy and Eternity.

ଔ

Praise the Lord from the heavens; praise him in the heights.
Praise him, all you his angels; give praise, all you his hosts.
Praise him, sun and moon; praise him, all shining stars.
Praise him, highest heavens, you waters above the heavens.

Let them all praise the Lord's name;
for he commanded and they were created,
Assigned them their station forever, set an order that will
never change. Praise the Lord from the earth, you sea monsters
and all the deeps of the sea; Lightning and hail, snow and thick
clouds, storm wind that fulfills his command;

Mountains and all hills, fruit trees and all cedars;

Animals wild and tame, creatures that crawl; and birds
that fly; Kings of the earth and all peoples, princes and all who
govern on earth; Young men and women too,
old and young alike.

Let them all praise the Lord's name, for his name alone is
exalted, His majesty above earth and heaven.
(Psalm 148)

PRESENCE I

St. Ignatius was spiritually illiterate for the first thirty years of life. His conversion was an awakening to his authentic character; his spiritual being. As he awakened, he exclaimed: "what is this new life we are living?" Indeed, it was a new life because he was beginning to glimpse life-as-a-whole. We are all called to conversion and awakening as was St. Ignatius. It is imperative that we awaken, for God lives and is *present* to us in the eternal *now*. Today is the time to wake from sleep (Rom 13: 11). We can find God and love only in the *present moment*. Let the awesomeness of this truth create wonder in your heart. Ponder its meaning. Give thanks.

Pray to stay awake.
Pray to cultivate an attentive heart.
Pray for continued mind/heart awakening.
Pray that Christ's spirit illuminate all your
thoughts, words and deeds.
Awaken to Creation, Presence, Memory, Mercy and Eternity.

Let the words of my mouth and the thought of my heart
find favor before you,
O lord, my rock and my redeemer.
(Psalm 19:15)

PRESENCE II

Most of us spend a significant amount of time fretting over the past and worrying about the future. It is not easy to stay awake and live in the present where God's grace and Spirit enliven. Yet it is essential because we can't open ourselves to God and God's graces when we fret about the past or worry about the future (Mt. 6:34). We must strive to anchor our attention in the present and invite God to help us accomplish this spiritual goal.

It is not possible to achieve this level of attentiveness *without* God's help. God will help us do what we, alone and unaided, cannot do for ourselves. Opening to the graces of the present moment is a life-long spiritual goal that Christ will help you achieve. But it will only be in the kingdom-to-come that we will be *fully present*. Only then will our hearts no longer be divided because they will be made whole by Christ's reconciling love. Let the awesomeness of this truth create wonder in your heart. Ponder its meaning. Give thanks.

Pray to stay awake.
Pray to cultivate an attentive heart.
Pray for continued mind/heart awakening.
Pray that Christ's Spirit illuminate all your
thoughts, words and deeds. Awaken to
Creation, Presence, Memory, Mercy and Eternity.

؃

On you I depend from birth;
from my mother's womb you are my strength.
My mouth shall declare your justice,
day by day your salvation.
O God, you have taught me from my youth,
and till the present I proclaim your wondrous deeds.
(Psalm 71:6, 15-17)

PRESENCE III

There are two ways of cultivating presence. One is to become aware of what you are feeling and thinking. The other is to actively cultivate awareness of something specific beyond a simple awareness of thoughts and feelings. The first way is simply recognizing *what* is happening in your mind and heart. The second way is directing your awareness to something that stirs up your gratitude as you are present to it.

In John's first letter, he affirms that love (sometimes translated "gratitude") casts out fear: "There is no fear in love, but perfect love drives out fear because fear has to do with punishment, and so one who fears is not yet perfect in love." (1 Jn 4:18). Those who specialize in neuroscience point out that fear and gratitude/appreciation cannot exist simultaneously in our minds. Cultivating love, gratitude and appreciation pushes fear out of our consciousness. Science seems to be catching up with Gospel truths!

So strive to simply be aware of what is happening in your mind and heart. But also strive to intentionally direct your conscious awareness to love, gratitude and appreciation for your awareness—for your very existence!. Awareness leads to healing but remember we will only be fully aware and fully well in the kingdom-to-come. Let the awesomeness of this truth create gratitude in your heart. Ponder its meaning. *Consciously* give thanks.

Pray to cultivate a spirit of gratitude in your awareness of presence.
Pray to cultivate an attentive, grateful heart. Pray for continued
mind/heart awakening to all God's gifts. Pray that the Holy Spirit
illuminate all your thoughts, words and deeds.
Awaken to Creation, Presence, Memory, Mercy and Eternity.

 C3

I will give thanks to you, O LORD, with all my heart,
for you have heard the words of my mouth;
in the presence of the angels I will sing your praise;
I will worship at your holy temple
and give thanks to your name.
In the sight of the angels I will sing your praises, Lord.
(Psalm 138:1-2)

PRESENCE IV

As Director of Retreats at Georgetown University, I realized how difficult it was for most people to take time away for a "silent" retreat. The most common excuse 'not to attend' went something like this: "Father, I am not the silent type so this would not work for me." I soon discovered that the true motivation behind this response was anxiety about what a person might discover in the time of silence.

Most of us can live life on the surface, never having the time to allow our deep thoughts and feelings to arise. We are afraid of what we might discover. Or we are afraid of what God might ask of us.

We must remember that this fear does not come from God - it comes from the enemy of our human nature. Entering "presence" necessarily means that we allow the Spirit to enter into the depths of our lives: our memories, feelings, and thoughts. It also means we must slow down enough at least once daily to allow the stirrings of our heart's deepest truths to be revealed. We must resist the fear that keeps us from slowing down and entering into our hearts, that deep place where God meets us. Be Not Afraid!

Pray this to resist the fear that keeps you from entering the depths of your heart's memories, feelings and thoughts. Pray for a spirit of courage to enter into presence. Pray that the Holy Spirit illuminate all your thoughts, words and deeds. Awaken to Creation, Presence, Memory, Mercy and Eternity.

ॐ

No evil shall befall you,
nor shall affliction come near your tent,
For to his angels he has given command about you,
that they guard you in all your ways.
(Psalm 91:10-11)

PRESENCE V

Recently, I ran across a travel brochure from the 1950's promoting Florida for winter vacations. The hook: "we have more healthful UV rays than anywhere else in the United States." Of course I burst into horrified laughter knowing those *healthful UV rays* were giving cancer to millions of people.

Today, we bathe ourselves in the rays from TVs, computers, iPhones, gaming platforms and other cyber-screens that have promised to connect us to the world. There is growing scientific consensus that our prolonged screens exposure has its own kind of cancerous effect on our consciousness.

We are turning inwards and away from friends, relationships and God as we get hooked on our virtual realities. We need to cultivate *technology-free zones* in our lives so our consciousness of God—our feelings, awareness, and thoughts—can be protected and allowed room to breathe. We need to realize that technology, while giving us the illusion of being present to the world via the extreme amount of data we consume daily, is eroding presence and consciousness at an alarming rate.

Pray that the Holy Spirit illuminate all your thoughts, words and deeds so that you can personally encounter Christ in his passion and so find Him in your life story as Creation, Presence, Memory, Mercy and Eternity.

ɔ8

*They divide my garments among them,
and for my vesture they cast lots.
But you, O LORD, be not far from me;
O my help, hasten to aid me.
My God, my God, why have you abandoned me?
(Psalm 22: 19-20)*

MEMORY I

Tradition affirms that human nature was *created* and *willed* by God to be a fusion of body and spirit. We are enfleshed spirits. As we begin five reflections on Memory, we first look at the physical organ called the brain that interacts with our spiritual self. And we should be amazed at what God as wrought!

Although the brain is only 1-2% of our body weight, this magnificent organ uses 15% of our blood flow, 20% of the air we breathe and 20-30% of the energy from the calories we consume. It has about 100,000 miles of functional nerve fibers wound tightly into a bundle no bigger than your two clenched fists. Its 100 billion neuron cells communicate with each other with up to a quadrillion connections, numbering several thousand times the total number of planets and suns in our Milky Way galaxy. Beyond our conscious perceptions, it manages hundreds of thousands of automatic functions per second that keep us standing straight, breathing, sensing, and responding to stress. There is no way for science to estimate the number of memories "recorded" here, but it could be in the trillions.

Pray that the Holy Spirit illuminate all your thoughts, words and deeds so that you can personally encounter Christ in your memories, He who is the source of all Creation, Presence, Memory, Mercy and Eternity.

○ଷ

*The stone which the builders rejected
has become the cornerstone.
By the LORD has this been done;
it is wonderful in our eyes.
This is the day the Lord has made; let us rejoice and be glad.
(Psalm 118: 22-24)*

MEMORY II

In his majestic Book X of The Confessions, St. Augustine affirms that everything we have ever done is held in our memory. Augustine uses the classical understanding that memories are held in our five senses: vision, touch, smell, taste and hearing. The Latin word veritas is commonly translated as our English word "truth." But one of the Greek words commonly used for the Latin *veritas* is *aletheia*. It means that which is "unconcealed" or perhaps, that which is unforgotten. Yet we experience, like Augustine, that our remembering can be quite faulty. So how can we discern what is true in things unforgotten?

Perhaps we can again look to Augustine, who concludes that God is not in our memory as a piece of data. God is there by an act of making Himself known to our human nature. As God willed human nature to be a fusion of body and spirit, God also wills that we be capable of experiencing and perceiving the Divinity within us. So even in our imperfect remembering, it will be God who will enable us to sort out the true from the false in those memories. And it is God who reveals the truth to us that compels us to make our own confession of faith.

Oh God, we ask you to enlighten the eyes of our minds, so that we can discern the true from the false in our great storehouse of memories. We pray that we can find you and your Son, Jesus, in our human experience. Help us to do this so that all our thoughts, words and deeds reveal your Creation, Presence, Memory, Mercy and Eternity.

ભ

Sing praise to the LORD, you his faithful ones,
and give thanks to his holy name.
For his anger lasts but a moment;
a lifetime, his good will.
At nightfall, weeping enters in,
but with the dawn, rejoicing.
(Psalm 30: 11-12)

MEMORY III

In the last two reflections, we have explored the science and the mystery of memory. For this lesson, we reflect on the challenge of taking time, daily, to listen to our memories (our hearts). C.S. Lewis reminds us that a major tactic of the one St. Ignatius calls "the enemy of human nature" is getting people to forget that God exists. This is accomplished by creating a world of noise and overwork. Thomas Merton also noted the "violence of hyper activism" as a major evil in the modern world.

We have technology that is supposed to save us time, yet it appears to makes us more scattered and distracted—and it creates more work! We have a very hard time slowing down to do the one thing in life that produces the most fruit: listening to God speak to us in the silence of our hearts. Even Jesus reprimanded Martha for her overwork and commended Mary who was sitting at the feet of the master (Lk 10:38-42).

The purpose of the once or twice daily *Sacred Story* prayer is to slow down, and attune to our memories—our hearts. We are invited to step out of our hyper-active and distracted lives, and enter the stream of the eternal. In reflecting back over our day, we are asking for grace to "see, feel and understand" in our memories (our hearts) where God was present, and where we have been tempted to depart from the ways of God. The goal in this contemplative rest is to allow our relationship with Christ to grow, daily, in our own lives. What a small cost for a pearl of such value: fruit that endures to eternity!

Oh God, we ask you for the grace slow down and open our hearts to you, so we can find you in the memories from our day. Open us to see, feel and understand where we turn to you, and turn from you, so that our whole being might reveal your Creation, Presence, Memory, Mercy and Eternity.

Ↄ

Sing joyfully to the LORD, all you lands;
serve the LORD with gladness;
come before him with joyful song.
Know that the LORD is God;
he made us, his we are;
his people, the flock he tends.
The LORD is good:
his kindness endures forever,
and his faithfulness, to all generations.
(Psalm 100: 1-2: 3-5)

MEMORY IV

In the last three reflections, we have explored the science and the mystery of memory, as well as the challenges presented by a hyper-active culture in slowing down long enough to "listen" to our hearts. For this lesson, we reflect on Memory's "first level." During our 15-minute prayer, we ask for God's grace to "recall" the most recent thoughts, words and events of the past day or half-day.

St. Ignatius paused briefly every hour on the hour to attend to the thoughts, words and deeds of the previous hour. And he did this with an eye to the spiritual messages contained in the events. Quite amazing! This is how he became a master of discernment. Like Ignatius, once or twice a day you are invited to listen to your previous day or half-day, and recall the most significant "events" and/or spiritual movements you experienced. We really need God's grace for this "holy remembering" because we are trying to look at events and sift them for their spiritual content. This holy remembering will, by grace, help us begin to "see" the thoughts, words and deeds of our day (or half-day) with spiritual eyes. Remember how often Sacred Story emphasizes: *Wake up to your spiritual nature. Wake Up!*

You have already begun to discover that all your thoughts, words and deeds have spiritual significance. This daily or half-daily "holy remembering" will enable you, by grace, to better see the spiritual forces that help you or hinder your growth, and to better see the outlines of your life as *Sacred Story.*

Oh God, we ask your help for our daily holy remembering. May we begin to see more clearly, in all our thoughts, words and deeds, that which moves us closer to you and also that which removes us from your presence. We ask a measure of grace each moment so that gradually, all our thoughts, words and deeds are shaped by your
Creation, Presence, Memory, Mercy and Eternity.

ↂ

Let them make known your might to the children of Adam, and the glorious splendor of your kingdom. Your kingdom is a kingdom for all ages, and your dominion endures through all generations. (Psalm 145: 12-13)

MEMORY V

In the last four reflections, we have explored the science and the mystery of memory, the challenges presented by a hyperactive culture, and the complexities of Memory's "first level." This time we reflect on Memory's "second level," which extends back into our past.

In order to understand our thoughts, words and deeds in the present, we must have some awareness of how they link to events from our past history. And to understand our past history it is important to understand that our subconscious awareness holds 99.999% of what we have experienced in life. Events in the present trigger our subconscious memories, which can operate at approximately one million times the speed of our conscious awareness. We "unconsciously" interpret our conscious awareness based on past experiences.

When we enter our 15 minute daily prayer, we need to ask for God's grace to remember thoughts, words, and deeds from our past day or half-day, in and of themselves, but also in light of our past history. We seek God's grace to help us dismantle present sinful, destructive, and addictive thoughts, words, and deeds that have their roots in our early "story."

This daily or half-daily "holy remembering", facilitated by God's grace, can help you begin to link your present and your past history. Jesus will make your "holy remembering" bear fruit. Jesus is the same yesterday today and forever, and He will ensure you find healing and peace for your past, present and into your future.

Oh God, we ask your help for our daily holy remembering of the present and the past. May we begin to see more clearly, in all our thoughts, words and deeds, that which moves us closer to you and also that which removes us from your presence. We ask a measure of grace each moment so that gradually, all our thoughts, words and deeds are shaped by your Creation, Presence, Memory, Mercy and Eternity.

ॐ

May the nations be glad and exult because you rule the peoples in equity; the nations on the earth you guide. May the peoples praise you, O God; may all the peoples praise you! May God bless us, and may all the ends of the earth fear him!
(Psalm 67: 5, 6, 8)

MERCY I

We begin a series of five reflections on the theme of Mercy; the fourth meditation in our *Sacred Story* prayer. In the last three meditations (Creation, Presence & Memory) we have been seeking God's grace to weave a story from attending to our life-experiences once or twice daily These experiences and/or events all lead to the Mercy of God.

Mercy is a quality of God's love that encompasses compassion, tenderness and patience. Saint Pope John Paul II's first encyclical was titled: *Dives et Misericordia; Rich in Mercy.* The Holy Father opens with this sentence: *It is "God, who is rich in mercy" (Eph 2:4) whom Jesus Christ has revealed to us as Father: it is His very Son who, in Himself, has manifested Him and made Him known to us (Cf. Jn 1:18; Heb 1: 1f).*

God's Mercy is revealed throughout scripture. It is revealed as well in holy devotions like the Sacred Heart of Christ and Divine Mercy. It is a quality of God's love that softens the fear and anxiety of those who have sinned and those in trouble and those who need, more than anything else, compassion, tenderness and patience.

As we begin our reflections on the meditation of Mercy, search your heart for what experiences, sufferings, failings and sins in your life draw you to desire—to need—the Mercy of God to be showered upon you. What are they? Name them and bring them to Jesus who is Divine Mercy, Sacred Heart and the Compassion of God the Father.

Oh God, you are merciful and compassionate. Help us to trust your merciful love. May we experience, more each day, why we need Your Mercy, as well as the experience of its graces in our hearts. In this we can be Your presence in the world and reveal Your Mercy to others so that all our thoughts, words and deeds are shaped by Your
Creation, Presence, Memory, Mercy and Eternity.

ᴄ₰

For king of all the earth is God;
sing hymns of praise.
God reigns over the nations,
God sits upon his holy throne.
(Psalm 47: 8-9)

MERCY II

We reflected first on Mercy as a quality of God's love that encompasses compassion, tenderness and patience. Next we are invited to consider this unique quality of love in light of our failings and sin. God created human persons as sinless, perfect beings. Our rejection of God, and the sin and death that resulted, inspired God's Mercy to help humanity regain what was lost.

God's Mercy goes beyond merely tolerating my sinful identity—an identity which results from sin's evolution in my history, my story. God's Mercy, through Jesus' life, death and resurrection, has destroyed sin and death. In this Mercy, I have the courage to reject my sinful identity, no matter how it has defined me, and by the Spirit's power, find forgiveness of my sins, becoming a new creation in Christ.

Jesus does not merely tolerate the woman caught in adultery, but by showing Mercy, gives her the strength to "go...and do not sin anymore." (Jn 8: 11). It is God's Mercy in Jesus that gives us the courage to change long-standing patterns of sin that have marred our human nature. And it is the power of Jesus' death and resurrection that wipes away the effects of that sinful identity and transforms us, redeeming our fallen human nature.

Oh God, you are merciful and compassionate. Send us your Spirit and inspire us to turn to you at all times. Give us a personal knowledge of your Merciful love in light of our need to be forgiven and transformed into a new creation. Help us to not lose hope due to our broken human nature, but to trust in your forgiveness to be transformed into a new creation. Help us, so that all our thoughts, words and deeds are shaped by Your Creation, Presence, Memory, Mercy and Eternity.

○3

*If you take away their breath, they perish
and return to their dust.
When you send forth your spirit, they are created,
and you renew the face of the earth.
Lord, send out your Spirit, and
Renew the face of the earth.
(Psalm 104: 31, 34)*

MERCY III

In the last two reflections we have examined Mercy as a manifestation of God's love in response to our sinfulness and weakness. This time we focus on the daily Christian labor of accepting God's Mercy in light of our own personal sinfulness and failures.

Jesus' mission was to end death's reign by the forgiveness of our sins. When we allow ourselves to encounter Jesus as Divine Physician, Redeemer and God's Mercy for our own sins and failings, we are truly meeting Him. In surrendering our sinfulness to Jesus, who alone can forgive us, we are giving Christ Jesus a gift of great significance. In this act we are truly accepting the reason He lived, died and rose again.

There is no greater gift He wants to give to us than to forgive us of our sins. And we should not delay in daily offering our weaknesses and sins to Him for His Mercy. St. Ignatius wanted us to *feel* the depths of our sinfulness so we would know *why* we need a Savior and why we can't save ourselves. St. Therese of Lisieux learned to trust God and would scour her life daily to see what new pattern of sin and failing she could offer to God for Mercy and healing.

We spend far too much time justifying our sins and failings and in so doing, we waste the precious gift of Mercy. We must overcome our tendency to justify our sins, and instead learn to throw ourselves on God's Mercy. Pope Francis said in his very first Sunday Angelus message: *God never tires of forgiving us. We get tired of asking God for forgiveness.* Ask to know your sins and failings. Then ask the Divine Physician to heal you and forgive you. This is why we *daily* come to the Lord Jesus in our *Sacred Story* prayer and ask for His Mercy.

Lord Jesus, wake us up. Help us to stop justifying our sins and instead, come to you for MERCY so our lives and all our thoughts, words and deeds are shaped by Your Creation, Presence, Memory, Mercy and Eternity.

ଔ

When I behold your heavens, the work of your fingers, the moon and the stars which you set in place —
What is man that you should be mindful of him, or the son of man that you should care for him?
(Psalm 8: 4-5)

MERCY IV

Previously we have pondered God's love as Mercy and the Gospel mandate that we honestly identify our sinfulness and ask for His Mercy. This reflection briefly explores how we who are forgiven by Mercy are called to offer Mercy to those who sin against us.

Original Sin unleashed an evil evolution in human history. Everyone has become an unwitting victim of this evil. Yet to one degree or another, we also all participate in it. The most profound manifestation of God's Love offered in Christ is the forgiveness of our sins. He invites and requires that we, who are forgiven, also offer that same Mercy and forgiveness to those who have sinned against us.

We can't withhold our Mercy because of injustice committed against us. We have been given a supreme example by Christ who forgave whose who betrayed, tortured and killed Him; the Son of Justice. "Father forgive them, they know not what they do." (Lk 23: 34).

Search your history for those people that you have withheld your Mercy from because of your *justified* anger. Realize that Christ has demolished all our arguments to hold on to anger for those who sinned against us by forgiving those who betrayed him (Scribes, Pharisees, disciples, torturers, and all sinners). Pray to be given the knowledge of where you are being called to offer Mercy for these persons who hurt you. Pray too for the grace to be able to offer it freely. God will hear your prayer and give you the grace you need *if* you ask for His help!

Lord Jesus, wake us up to those people whom we fail to offer your Mercy, due to our belief that we are justified in our ongoing anger. Help us to offer your Mercy to all so that we become your presence in the world and find in You our Creation, Presence, Memory, Mercy and Eternity.

ॐ

Yours is princely power in the day of your birth, in holy splendor;
before the daystar, like the dew, I have begotten you.
The LORD has sworn, and he will not repent:
You are a priest forever, according to the order of Melchizedek.
(Psalm 110: 3-4)

MERCY V

God created the world through Love and for Love. Mercy is God's response to humankind's rejection of His Love, that Love which was our gift and inheritance. Mercy and the forgiveness of sins it enfolds are the only hope for the salvation of the world. For God desires that all be saved, as we hear both in the book of Wisdom and John's Gospel. God's Mercy knows no boundaries!

But you spare all things, because they are yours, O Ruler and Lover of souls, for your imperishable spirit is in all things! (Ws 11: 26)

Everything that the Father gives me will come to me, and I will not reject anyone who comes to me, because I came down from heaven not to do my own will but the will of the one who sent me. And this is the will of the one who sent me that I should not lose anything of what he gave me, but that I should raise it [on] the last day. For this is the will of my Father, that everyone who sees the Son and believes in him may have eternal life, and I shall raise him [on] the last day." (Jn 6: 37-40)

Lord Jesus, help us to daily accept your awesome gift of Mercy.
Help us to daily offer Mercy to all those we meet, especially those
who have hurt us in any way. In this, may we help reveal your
Love to the world in Jesus Christ, He who is our
Creation, Presence, Memory, Mercy and Eternity.

ଔ

Sing praise to the LORD, you his faithful ones,
and give thanks to his holy name.
For his anger lasts but a moment;
a lifetime, his good will.
At nightfall, weeping enters in,
but with the dawn, rejoicing.
(Psalm 30: 5-6)

ETERNITY I

Sacred Story prayer calls our attention daily to Eternity. Doing so makes us aware of what is truly valuable in life. Over these next five reflections, we will pause briefly and notice some of the important things Eternity inspires. For this reflection, we realize that focusing on Eternity helps us realize this life is transient.

With our first-ever pope named Francis, we are reminded that St. Francis of Assisi regularly prayed to God in the presence of a skull. By doing so he daily recalled that he was dust and to dust he would return. St. Ignatius said in the Constitutions:

"For our profession requires that we be prepared and very much ready for whatever is enjoined upon us in our Lord and at whatsoever time, without asking for or expecting any reward in this present and transitory life, but hoping always for that life which lasts for eternity, through God's supreme mercy."

When we recall our mortality in contemplation of Eternity, we keep our final destination clearly in view: God, who is our source and our Eternity.

Lord Jesus, help us to daily remember that we have been created from the dust, and to dust we shall return. Yet we do not despair, because You are our hope and our Eternity.
May we your restore in us life's true meaning so that in all our thoughts and words and deeds, we will see Christ who is our Creation, Presence, Memory, Mercy and Eternity.

ᚙ

I acknowledged my sin to you,
my guilt I covered not.
I said, "I confess my faults to the LORD,"
and you took away the guilt of my sin.
You are my shelter; from distress you will preserve me;
with glad cries of freedom you will ring me round.
(Psalm 32: 5,7)

ETERNITY II

We reflected first on how awareness of Eternity helps us to realize that life on this earth is short. Now we reflect that this transience can open us to see each day as a spiritual event that transcends time and material concerns. Knowing that life has a fixed end, I am freed to search for life's spiritual meaning and help others do the same.

Therefore I tell you, do not worry about your life, what you will eat [or drink], or about your body, what you will wear. Is not life more than food and the body more than clothing? Look at the birds in the sky; they do not sow or reap, they gather nothing into barns, yet your heavenly Father feeds them. Are not you more important than they? Can any of you by worrying add a single moment to your life-span? Why are you anxious about clothes? Learn from the way the wild flowers grow. They do not work or spin. But I tell you that not even Solomon in all his splendor was clothed like one of them. If God so clothes the grass of the field, which grows today and is thrown into the oven tomorrow, will he not much more provide for you, O you of little faith? So do not worry and say, 'What are we to eat?' or

'What are we to drink?' or 'What are we to wear?' All these things the pagans seek. Your heavenly Father knows that you need them all. But seek first the kingdom (of God) and his righteousness, and all these things will be given you besides.(Mt 6: 25-33)

> *Lord Jesus, help us to daily remember that worry is truly a fruitless use of our precious time. Help us to look to your Eternity and the Love you have for us.*
> *May our awareness of your eternal Love open our hearts -hourly, daily, weekly, yearly-to you who are Creation, Presence, Memory, Mercy and Eternity.*

℘

> *O God, you are my God whom I seek; for you my flesh pines and my soul thirsts like the earth, parched, lifeless and without water.*
> *Thus have I gazed toward you in the sanctuary to see your power and your glory, For your kindness is a greater good than life; my lips shall glorify you. You are my help, and in the shadow of your wings I shout for joy. My soul clings fast to you; your right hand upholds me.*
> *(Psalm 63: 2,3-4, 7-8)*

ETERNITY III

Having looked at Eternity we have pondered how it reveals life's transience and how that helps us see each day as a spiritual event. Now we briefly reflect that a daily focus on Eternity keeps our heart focused on the One who is our source and our final end, God.

We had complete intimacy with God at our creation. We lived in a paradise of loving relationship with God, each other and with the created order. The tragedy of Original Sin is that it ended that perfect paradise of love, bringing grief, sickness and death into human history. Eternity is our reminder that Christ has come to restore what was lost, and open for us the path back to complete intimacy with God in the Kingdom to come.

*Lord Jesus, Eternity with you and the Father is our promise and
our hope. Help us to keep our minds and hearts focused on
Eternity and you who are
Creation, Presence, Memory, Mercy and Eternity.*

03

Therefore my heart is glad and my soul rejoices,
my body, too, abides in confidence
because you will not abandon my soul to the netherworld,
nor will you suffer your faithful one to undergo corruption.
You will show me the path to life,
fullness of joys in your presence,
the delights at your right hand forever.
(Psalm 16: 9-10, 11)

ETERNITY IV

Eternity is our focus and now we briefly reflect that our every thought, word and deed has significance for the salvation history of the world and for all of eternity.

Some years ago, Mother Theresa proposed that just giving someone a smile instead of a frown can change things: "Peace begins with a smile." Similarly, every one of our thoughts, words and deeds contributes to God's mission of redemption, or they work to frustrate this mission. We might also remind ourselves that our thoughts, words and deeds can be motivated by the grace of God or by the deceptions of the enemy of our human nature.

Our thoughts, words and deeds—every single one of them—are of great significance not only for us, but for Christ's work of redemption. His redemption is already ushering in a new heavens and a new earth. Every thought, word and deed, is thus linked to Eternity.

Perhaps you can stop and just say aloud: "every one of my

thoughts words and deeds can work with you Christ, or against You. Lord, help me wake up to this truth."

Lord Jesus, help me awaken more each day, and allow every thought, word and deed of mine work with your Love. May every thought, word and deed of mine produce fruit that endures to Eternity. May I realize the significance of everything I do, and live for your Kingdom through my prayer in Creation, Presence, Memory, Mercy and Eternity.

ᘓ

*Hear now, all you who fear God, while I declare what he has done for me.
Blessed be God who refused me not my prayer or his kindness!
(Psalm 66: 20)*

181

ETERNITY V

We conclude our reflections on Eternity by a focus on what our Eternity might be like. St. Paul says: "Now we are seeing a dim reflection in a mirror, but then we shall be seeing face to face" (1 Cor 13:12). Echoing the prophet Isaiah, Paul reminds us "Eye has not seen, and ear has not heard what God has prepared for those who love him" (1 Cor 2: 9).

There will be a new heavens and a new Earth. Our immortality will be restored with an Eternity of joy and communion with Father, Son and Spirit and with all the elect. "He will wipe every tear from their eyes, and there shall be no more death or mourning, wailing or pain, [for] the old order has passed away" (Rev 21: 4). The experience of love shared and given in the Father's Kingdom increases without limit.

There will always be new depths of love and joy to experience for all Eternity. Jesus, the Divine Physician speaks directly to us when

He says: "Do not let your hearts be troubled. You have faith in God; have faith also in me. In my Father's house there are many dwelling places. And if I go and prepare a place for you, I will come back again and take you to myself, so that where I am you also may be." (Jn 14: 1, 3).

Lord Jesus, you have won the victory over death and loneliness. Please help me to open to your love each day to begin serving you and your Kingdom. Help me to live my life so it produces fruit enduring to Eternity by opening to Creation, Presence, Memory, Mercy and Eternity.

ଔ

*"For God will save Zion
and rebuild the cities of Judah.
The descendants of his servants shall inherit it,
and those who love his name shall inhabit it."
(Psalm 69: 37)*

LIST OF PHOTOGRAPHS[5]

---

[5] The photos, excepting the two from Wikipedia and the ones from San Chapelle, Paris, were taken by the author using an iPhone 4S and 6.

[6] All photos taken in Laguna Hills are from the home of Tim and Steph Busch and their collection of religious art.

[7] Palisades photos taken at Archbishop Alex Brunet Retreat Center

[8] Photos from Lafayette are at the Trappist Monastery of Our Lady of Guadalupe

[9] The pictures from San Chapelle are from the carvings at the main portal entry to this Gothic masterpiece and were taken with a Nikon 6000 by the author.

67. Winter Sun, Seattle WA

70. Church of the Gesu, Cleveland OH

73. Christ our Light, Oakland CA

76. Morning Storm, Seattle WA

79. Earth's Mantle, Olympic National Park, WA

82. Sun Break, Port Stewart, Northern Ireland

85. Irish Fog, Coleraine, Northern Ireland

88. Our Lady, Santa Rosa CA

91. Forest Stairway, Arboretum-Seattle WA

94. Gnarled Tree, Arboretum-Seattle WA

97. Paradise, San Chapelle, Paris

100. Ancient Antlers, National Bison Reserve MT

103. Pieta, St. James Cathedral-Seattle WA

106. Mystic Window, Santa Rosa CA

109. Lilly of the Valley, Seattle WA

112. St. Ignatius, Spokane WA

115. Winter Rain, Seattle WA

121. Galaxy, Wikipedia

124. Earth, Wikipedia

127. Divine Touch, Seattle WA

130. Creation, San Chapelle, Paris

133. Christmas Family, Laguna Hills CA

135. Morning Light, Colombia Gorge, WA

138. Mother's Chair, Black Lake, ID

141. Spring Thaw, Olympic National Park WA

144. Mother and Child, Laguna Hills, CA

147. Storm, Colombia Gorge WA

150. Spring, Arboretum, Seattle WA

153. Christ Cathedral, Anaheim CA

156. Gesu Church, Cleveland OH

ABOUT THE AUTHOR

Fr. William Watson, S.J., D. Min., has spent over thirty years developing Ignatian programs and retreats. Fr. Watson has served as: Director of Retreat Programs at Georgetown University; Vice President for Mission at Gonzaga University; and Provincial Assistant for International Ministries for the Oregon Province of the Society of Jesus. He holds Masters Degrees in Divinity and Pastoral Studies, respectively (1986; Weston Jesuit School of Theology, Cambridge Massachusetts). He received his Doctor of Ministry degree in 2009 from The Catholic University of America (Washington D.C.).

In the spring of 2011 Fr. Watson launched the non-profit Sacred Story Institute, to bring Ignatian Spirituality to Catholics of all ages and walks of life. The Sacred Story Institute is promoting third millennium evangelization for the Society of Jesus and the Church by using the time-tested *Examination of Conscience* of St. Ignatius.

Sacred Story Press
Seattle, Washington, USA
sacredstorypress.com

Sacred Story Press explores dynamic new dimensions of classic Ignatian spirituality, based on St. Ignatius' Conscience Examen in the *Sacred Story* prayer method pioneered by Fr. Bill Watson, S.J. We are creating a new class of spiritual resources. Our publications are research-based, authentic to the Catholic Tradition and designed to help individuals achieve integrated, spiritual growth and holiness of life.

We Request Your Feedback

The Sacred Story Institute welcomes feedback on all our publications. Contact us via email or letter. Give us ideas, suggestions and inspirations for how to make better resources for Catholics and Christians of all ages and walks of life.

For bulk orders and group discounts, contact us:
admin-team@sacredstory.net
Sacred Story Institute & Sacred Story Press
1401 E. Jefferson Suite 405
Seattle, Washington, 98122

SACRED STORY ROSARY

AN IGNATIAN WAY TO PRAY THE MYSTERIES

WILLIAM M. WATSON, SJ
ART BY MARY GRACE THUL, OP

Coming Spring 2015 in English and Spanish

Made in the USA
Monee, IL
10 February 2020